Forecasting and Recognizing
Business Cycle Turning Points

NATIONAL BUREAU OF ECONOMIC RESEARCH

Studies in Business Cycles

Forecasting and Recognizing
Business Cycle Turning Points

RENDIGS FELS

and

C. ELTON HINSHAW

NATIONAL BUREAU OF ECONOMIC RESEARCH

NEW YORK 1968

Distributed by COLUMBIA UNIVERSITY PRESS

NEW YORK AND LONDON

RELATION OF THE DIRECTORS TO THE WORK AND PUBLICATIONS OF THE NATIONAL BUREAU OF ECONOMIC RESEARCH

1. The object of the National Bureau of Economic Research is to ascertain and to present to the public important economic facts and their interpretation in a scientific and impartial manner. The Board of Directors is charged with the responsibility of ensuring that the work of the National Bureau is carried on in strict conformity with this object.

2. To this end the Board of Directors shall appoint one or more Directors of Research.

3. The Director or Directors of Research shall submit to the members of the Board, or to its Executive Committee, for their formal adoption, all specific proposals concerning researches to be instituted.

4. No report shall be published until the Director or Directors of Research shall have submitted to the Board a summary drawing attention to the character of the data and their utilization in the report, the nature and treatment of the problem involved, the main conclusions, and such other information as in their opinion would serve to determine the suitability of the report for publication in accordance with the principles of the National Bureau.

5. A copy of any manuscript proposed for publication shall also be submitted to each member of the Board. For each manuscript to be so submitted a special committee shall be appointed by the President, or at his designation by the Executive Director, consisting of three Directors selected as nearly as may be one from each general division of the Board. The names of the special manuscript committee shall be stated to each Director when the summary and report described in paragraph (4) are sent to him. It shall be the duty of each member of the committee to read the manuscript. If each member of the special committee signifies his approval within thirty days, the manuscript may be published. If each member of the special committee has not signified his approval within thirty days of the transmittal of the report and manuscript, the Director of Research shall then notify each member of the Board, requesting approval or disapproval of publication, and thirty additional days shall be granted for this purpose. The manuscript shall then not be published unless at least a majority of the entire Board and a two-thirds majority of those members of the Board who shall have voted on the proposal within the time fixed for the receipt of votes on the publication proposed shall have approved.

6. No manuscript may be published, though approved by each member of the special committee, until forty-five days have elapsed from the transmittal of the summary and report. The interval is allowed for the receipt of any memorandum of dissent or reservation, together with a brief statement of his reasons, that any member may wish to express; and such memorandum of dissent or reservation shall be published with the manuscript if he so desires. Publication does not, however, imply that each member of the Board has read the manuscript, or that either members of the Board in general, or of the special committee, have passed upon its validity in every detail.

7. A copy of this resolution shall, unless otherwise determined by the Board, be printed in each copy of every National Bureau book.

(Resolution adopted October 25, 1926,
as revised February 6, 1933, and February 24, 1941)

Contents

Tables

Charts

Acknowledgments

We owe more than the usual debt of gratitude to Geoffrey H. Moore, who contributed valuable ideas; to Victor Zarnowitz, who is in charge of the research project on short-term business forecasting at the National Bureau of Economic Research; to other members of the staff reading committee, Phillip Cagan and Ilse Mintz, who made helpful comments; to Stephen Axilrod, who reviewed Hinshaw's manuscript; to James F. McRee, Jr., and Joan R. Tron, who edited the manuscript; to H. Irving Forman who drew the charts; to C. Richard Long and John Pilgrim, who served as research assistants; and to the Directors' reading committee, Walter D. Fisher, Marion B. Folsom, and Murray Shields. No one, we trust, will make the mistake of blaming any of them for the shortcomings of these papers.

The study of short-term forecasting, of which this is a part, was supported by grants to the National Bureau from Whirlpool Corporation, General Electric Company, Ford Motor Company Fund, U.S. Steel Corporation, and the Relm Foundation, as well as by other funds of the National Bureau.

Foreword

The two papers included in this volume appraise the past performance of selected organizations in recognizing peaks and troughs of business cycles. We normally use the word "recognizing" to mean the entire pattern beginning with the vague early awareness that analysts ordinarily develop of an impending cyclical turn through the successive stages of increasing certainty until they finally become sure that a turn has definitely occurred. At times, however, we find it useful to select a single point in the pattern, in which case we use as the criterion for recognition the time at which the analysts first decide that a turning point is more probable than not. In this narrower sense of the term, recognition may come either before or after business peaks and troughs.

Our papers are part of a larger project conducted at the National Bureau of Economic Research under the direction of Victor Zarnowitz, a project concerned with appraising short-term business forecasts. The process of recognition in the broad sense begins some time before cyclical turns and ends some time afterward. The part of it that precedes peaks and troughs involves forecasting on anybody's definition of the latter term. But the part that follows peaks and troughs involves forecasting also. To assert several months after the event that a cyclical peak has occurred is to forecast that the decline in business will continue long enough and far enough to qualify as a business cycle contraction.

My paper, besides a brief analysis of a previous study of recognition in the 1920's by Garfield V. Cox, is concerned with the forecasting record of ten publications in the vicinities of the eight peaks and troughs between 1948 and 1961. Hinshaw's paper, which is a revision of his Ph.D. dissertation at Vanderbilt University, appraises the recognition of cyclical turns by the Federal Open Market Committee for the seven cyclical turns between 1948 and 1960. Since Hinshaw did not have access to the Committee's minutes for 1961, he was unable to include the trough that occurred in that year. His standard for evaluating the FOMC's recognition record is the performance of eight of the publications in my study for the seven peaks and troughs in question.

Either paper can be read independently of the other. Since each paper ends with a section summarizing its conclusions, I shall only mention here a few highlights. Recognition in the narrow sense (the earliest time at which forecasters become convinced that a turn is more likely than not) was achieved by the eight principal publications in my study one month before troughs and three months after peaks on the average. There is little evidence that users of the leading indicators of the NBER recognized turns faster than other forecasters. Neither does the evidence reviewed by Hinshaw suggest that the FOMC's recognition record was particularly better than the others. A brief note on Hinshaw's subject by Mark H. Willes recently appeared in the *Journal of Finance*.[1] Although Willes found a somewhat longer recognition lag for the FOMC than Hinshaw, the conclusions of the two studies are similar.

After this report went to press, some further research was undertaken with respect to false signals. Preliminary results indicate a need to modify some of our conclusions.

A stern test of forecasters' skill in recognizing turning points occurs in those years when the American economy experiences a hesitation or pause that does not quite qualify as a business cycle contraction. Such hesitations occurred in 1947, 1951, 1956, 1962, and 1967. To avoid recognition of turns that do not occur is just as much the mark of a good forecaster as to recognize genuine turns promptly.

Although our work on these periods is not yet completed, the results so far suggest the following conclusions:

1. None of the forecasters in my sample deserves to be called the "best." The publication labeled "best" in the various charts had the highest scores for accuracy of dating at both peaks and troughs and the highest scores for degree of certainty at troughs, though not at peaks. But it tended to sound false alarms more frequently than the rest.

2. Those relying heavily on business cycle indicators tended to give more false signals than the others. This finding adds to the evidence that an eclectic approach to recognition is desirable.

3. The preliminary results of the investigation of false signals by the publications in my sample indicate that, if the FOMC is regarded as a

[1] "The Inside Lags of Monetary Policy: 1952–1960," *Journal of Finance,* December 1967, pp. 591–593.

single forecaster, its recognition record is better than Hinshaw thought.[2] Hinshaw studied the FOMC for false signals during the entire period 1947–60. During that time, there was not a single instance of a false alarm. On the other hand, false alarms are by no means rare in the publications of my sample. By virtue of its consistently good perform-ance, the FOMC can be judged as one of the best of the eleven studied by Hinshaw and myself. Whether its record, in the words of Brunner and Meltzer, "can only be regarded as splendid" is for others to judge.

RENDIGS FELS

[2] If, however, the scores of the FOMC are regarded as averages of all those taking part in its discussions, then the relevant comparison is with the average of the publications in my sample. On this basis, the record of the FOMC is not obviously superior to that of the publications in my sample. Although in the cases of at least three of my ten, a single individual was mainly, if not entirely, re-sponsible for the forecasts, there is a presumption that in the other cases the forecast was made by a small group. Thus, what is the proper comparison to make is not clear.

PART I

The Recognition Patterns of Business Analysts

by RENDIGS FELS

1

Introduction

This paper reports on an investigation into the problem of forecasting and recognizing business cycle peaks and troughs. The word "recognizing" is used here to denote the pattern beginning with the vague early warnings forecasters usually give that the cyclical situation may be changing through the successive stages of increasing awareness until they finally confirm that a turn has definitely occurred.[1] In a sense, the entire process of recognition is one aspect of short-term business forecasting, though it is more usual to restrict the meaning of the phrase "forecasting cyclical turns" to the part of the recognition pattern that precedes the date of the peak or trough. The sooner a forecaster can give warning of a turnabout, even if the warning comes after the event, the more useful his forecasts will be. When he first gives warning, he may think a turning point is not probable. As time goes by, evidence for or against the hypothesis of a reversal builds up. In the case of a genuine turn, the forecaster eventually becomes certain. Confirmation that a turn has occurred can be useful for forecasting—is itself a forecast—if it can be achieved within six months (or sometimes even longer) after the peak or trough of the business cycle.[2]

[1] Terms like "recognition" and "recognition lag" are used in different senses in the literature. Kareken and Solow in a study of the Federal Reserve System defined recognition lag as the time between the need for action (viz., a cyclical peak or trough) and the time the Federal Reserve actually took action. (They assumed that the lag between recognition and decision was zero.) Brunner and Meltzer more or less followed the same usage. In these and other studies, recognition refers to a particular point in the recognition pattern rather than to the pattern as a whole. See John Kareken and Robert M. Solow, "Lags in Monetary Policy," in *Stabilization Policies,* prepared for the Commission on Money and Credit, Englewood Cliffs, N. J., 1963, pp. 62–65; and Karl Brunner and Allan H. Meltzer, *The Federal Reserve's Attachment to the Free Reserve Concept,* Subcommittee on Domestic Finance, House of Representatives, 88th Congress, 2d Session, Washington, 1964, pp. 37–47.

[2] Under the definition used by the NBER, a business cycle (expansion plus contraction) must last more than a year (Arthur F. Burns and Wesley C. Mitchell, *Measuring Business Cycles,* New York: National Bureau of Economic Research, 1946, p. 3). The shortest expansion on record lasted ten months, the

The purpose of this study is to describe and evaluate the recognition patterns of a representative group of business analysts. Following a review of a previous study for the 1920's by Garfield V. Cox, the paper discusses the forecasts of ten widely circulated publications, using a scoring system to evaluate their records in forecasting eight turning points since World War II. Though several different kinds of publications are represented, the ten do not constitute a random sample of forecasters. They have, however, put their analyses on record continuously for a substantial period of time, and their wide circulation suggests that they may have a significant influence on public opinion with respect to the state of the economy.

Geoffrey Moore, in discussing "the usual lag in recognizing revivals and recessions *that have already begun,"* has said, "this lag is clearly not negligible. If the user of statistical indicators could do no better than recognize contemporaneously the turns in general economic activity denoted by our reference dates, he would have a better record than most of his fellows." [3] This paper provides evidence bearing on Moore's hypothesis. It also throws some light on why recognition is difficult and on the comparative value of different forecasting methods.

Victor Zarnowitz has shown that one of the pervasive weaknesses of short-term business forecasting is its failure to predict changes in the direction of business activity (and sometimes its prediction of changes in direction that do not occur).[4] There evidently is no reliable way to forecast cyclical reversals even a few months in advance. This study shows that informed observers often do not know that a reversal is in the making until some months *after* the peak or trough.

shortest contraction seven months. The knowledge that a peak or trough has occurred leaves the domain of forecasting and enters that of historical fact perhaps half a year after the peak or trough itself, but this interval may be shorter or longer depending on economic developments, such as the rate of decline after the apparent peak or the vigor of recovery after the apparent trough. Before that time, confirmation implies a forecast of the direction and magnitude of change over the very short run.

The National Bureau has determined the dates of business cycle peaks and troughs historically for analytical purposes, often long after the fact. In the Department of Commerce monthly publication, *Business Cycle Developments,* which utilizes the National Bureau's dates, the position is taken that a peak or trough date will not be designated until at least six months after it has occurred (see p. 1 of each issue).

[3] Geoffrey H. Moore, *Business Cycle Indicators,* Princeton University Press for NBER, 1961, Vol. I, pp. 257–258 (Moore's italics).

[4] *An Appraisal of Short-Term Economic Forecasts,* Occasional Paper 104, National Bureau of Economic Research, New York, 1967, pp. 7 and 72–80.

2

Dates of Peaks and Troughs

Any attempt to determine how early forecasters gave warning of a particular turn and how prompt they were to confirm it requires knowing when the peak or trough of the business cycle came. The NBER chronology of reference cycle peaks and troughs serves this purpose well, despite the uncertainty attaching to particular dates. In some cases, such as 1932–33 and 1949, the NBER had to make a close decision because the trough was double-bottomed. In other cases, the decision was close, as between two or more contiguous months, because the turn was flat. On the basis of the revised NBER date for the 1929 peak (August), the recognition performance looks much better than it would have on the basis of the original date (June) given by Burns and Mitchell.[5] A more recent example is the August 1954 trough, where consideration of revised statistics may justify selection of an earlier date. In appraising recognition performances, account must be taken of all such circumstances. Table I-1 lists alternatives for fourteen peaks and troughs. Chart I-1 shows the behavior of five series representing economic aggregates in the vicinity of the eight peaks and troughs from 1948 through 1961. Note particularly the double bottom in 1949, the flat bottom in 1954, and the flat top in 1960. There are other circumstances making some turns inherently harder to recognize than others, but they are best discussed in the historical survey below.

[5] *Measuring Business Cycles,* p. 78.

TABLE I-1

Alternative Dates of Business Cycle Peaks and Troughs, 1919–61

NBER Date [a] (1)	Alternatives [b] (2)	References [c] (3)
Feb. 1961 (T)	None suggested	Zarnowitz, p. 189
May 1960 (P)	July	Cloos (cf. Zarnowitz, p. 188n)
Apr. 1958 (T)	None suggested	Zarnowitz, p. 189
July 1957 (P)	August	Trueblood, pp. 19 and 20n; Moore; Zarnowitz, p. 189
Aug. 1954 (T)	May–July	Trueblood, pp. 18–19; Zarnowitz, pp. 198–99
July 1953 (P)	None suggested	Zarnowitz, p. 189
Oct. 1949 (T)	July	Trueblood, pp. 17–18; Moore; Zarnowitz, pp. 186–88
Nov. 1948 (P)	October	Trueblood, p. 17; Moore; Zarnowitz, pp. 188–89
June 1938 (T)	May	Burns and Mitchell, p. 78
May 1937 (P)	June–August [d]	Burns and Mitchell, pp. 83 and 87
Mar. 1933 (T)	Summer 1932	Burns and Mitchell, p. 82
Aug. 1929 (P)	June	Burns and Mitchell, p. 78; Cox, p. 31
Nov. 1927 (T)	December	Burns and Mitchell, p. 78; Cox, p. 31
Oct. 1926 (P)	March 1927	Cox, p. 31
July 1924 (T)	None suggested	Cox, p. 31
May 1923 (P)	None suggested	Cox, p. 31
July 1921 (T)	March; September	Cox, p. 31; Burns and Mitchell, p. 78
Jan. 1920 (P)	March	Cox, p. 31
Mar. 1919 (T)	None suggested	Cox, p. 31

[a] *Business Cycle Developments,* September 1966, p. 65. This table omits the NBER peak of February 1945 and trough of October 1945.

[b] For 1938, 1929, 1927, and 1921, col. (2) includes the original dates given by Burns and Mitchell, p. 78, the corresponding dates in col. (1) being later revisions. Other dates in col. (2) are alternatives that have been suggested in the literature (except 1937, on which see note d). The older literature referred to by Burns and Mitchell on p. 108 has not been utilized, since it is not of interest for present purposes. This omission should be borne in mind in interpreting the entries for pre-World War II dates.

[c] Victor Zarnowitz, "On the Dating of Business Cycles," *Journal of Business,* April 1963, pp. 179–199; George W. Cloos, "How Good Are the National Bureau's Reference Dates?" *Journal of Business,* January 1963, pp. 14–32; Lorman C. Trueblood, "The Dating of Postwar Business Cycles," *Proceedings of the Business and Economics Section of the American Statistical Association,* Washington, D. C., 1961, pp. 16–26; Geoffrey H. Moore, "Discussion," *Proceedings of the Business and Economics Section of the American Statistical Association,* Washington, D. C., 1961, p. 34; Arthur F. Burns and Wesley C. Mitchell, *Measuring Business Cycles;* Garfield V. Cox, *An Appraisal of American Business Forecasts,* rev. edition, Chicago, 1930.

[d] The Barger-Klein estimate of GNP (available in Geoffrey H. Moore, ed., *Business Cycle Indicators,* Vol. II, p. 133) rose 5 per cent in the third quarter of 1937. Such a large rise is inconsistent with a date for the cyclical peak earlier than June. Since the quality of the GNP estimate is not high, there is no presumption that the NBER date is wrong, but for purposes of the present study the fact that two competent investigators long after the event produced such an estimate demonstrates how difficult it was for contemporary observers to recognize the turning point promptly.

CHART I-1

Five Aggregate Series, 1948–63

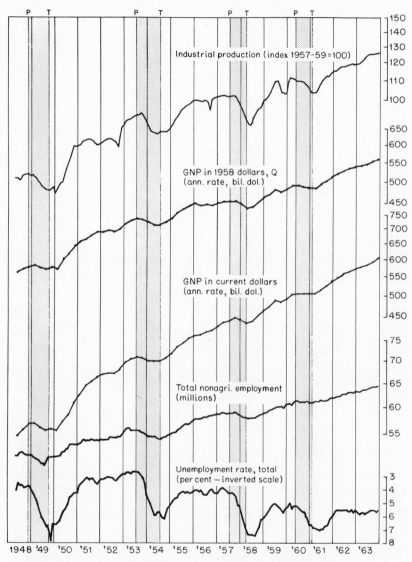

Shaded areas represent business cycle contractions (NBER dates).
SOURCE: Federal Reserve System; Department of Commerce; Bureau of Labor
Statistics.

3

The 1920's

Garfield V. Cox investigated six forecasting services during the 1920's.[6] Geoffrey H. Moore has devised methods of utilizing Cox's results to show the pattern of recognition of cyclical turning points and has applied the methods to 1919–27. The results of adding the 1929 peak to Moore's findings appear in Charts I-2 and I-3 below.

For each month of the period covered, Cox excerpted a brief quotation from each of six forecasting services, summarizing the service's view of the outlook. Cox then scored the quotations in two different ways, for warning of turning points and for general correctness. For purposes of the former, he determined dates of "major" upturns and downturns in the Annalist Index of Business Activity. These dates, fortunately, are in one-to-one correspondence with the NBER reference peaks and troughs for the decade in question.[7] Beginning with the earliest month in which any of the six forecasting services correctly predicted the turn, Cox rated each service for the month according to whether the direction of its prediction was right, wrong, or neutral (i.e., no forecast of a change in direction).[8] For example, on August 5, 1919,

[6] *An Appraisal of American Business Forecasts.* The second edition differs from the first, which was published in 1929, by incorporating part of the preliminary results of the author's study of 1928–29, published as "Another Year of Business Forecasts," *Journal of Business,* April 1930, pp. 151–170.

[7] *Ibid.,* p. 31. In three of the eight cases, the dates of Cox and the NBER are identical, in two cases the discrepancy is one month, in one case two months. (See Table I-1.) Cox's March 1921 upturn is four months earlier than the NBER's trough of July 1921. (The latter is a revision of the September 1921 date originally given.) Cox's March 1927 downturn is six months later than the NBER's October 1926 peak. (By "upturn" and "downturn," Cox meant approximately the same as what the NBER means by "trough" and "peak.") Even the large discrepancies seldom make a difference for present purposes (but cf. note 15 below).

[8] *Ibid.,* pp. 32–34. In some cases, notably 1926, the decision to begin the scoring with the first month in which any of the six services correctly anticipated the change of direction results in a bias (see Chart I-2). The scoring begins with September 1926, one month before the NBER peak. This fact implies that in the

CHART I-2

Recognition of Peaks and Troughs, Six Forecasting Services, 1919–29:
Direction of Change

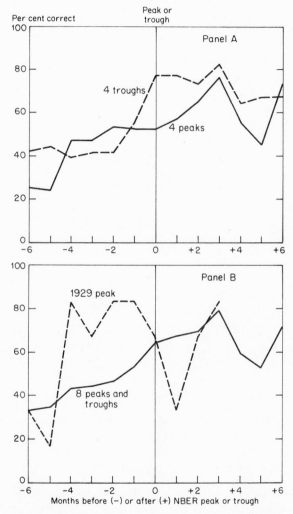

SOURCE: Garfield V. Cox, *An Appraisal of American Business Forecasts,*
revised ed., Chicago, 1930, pp. 85–90.

CHART I-3

*Correctness of Forecasts Made in the Vicinity of Peaks
and Troughs, Six Forecasting Services, 1919–29*

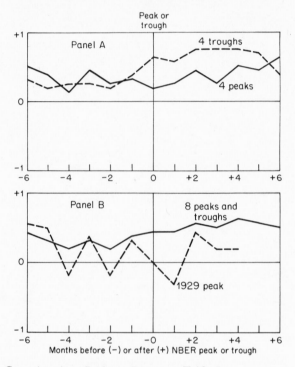

SOURCE: Cox, *American Business Forecasts,* Table I.

one forecaster said, "My opinion, briefly, is that there will be a distinct
shortage of labor this fall . . . and this shortage may continue into
next year; but that before long we are going to experience a real period

earlier months none of the forecasts was correct. In computing the averages for
months designated −6, −5, −4, −3, and −2 on the chart, 1926 has been
omitted from the denominator as well as the numerator. An alternative procedure
would be to consider all forecasters as having made incorrect forecasts for the
five months prior to September 1926. The average per cent of correct forecasts
six months before the four peaks would be reduced from 25 per cent to 13 per
cent, if all forecasts not available for this reason (including five at the January
1920 peak) were included in the denominator; five months before, from 17 per
cent to 13 per cent, etc.

With respect to anticipation of major turning points, Cox gave the forecasts
numerical scores for accuracy in predicting (1) amplitude of the expected movement in the changed direction and (2) the time of the turning point. These

of unemployment." [9] Cox rated this forecast correct, since it anticipated the downturn which he dated in March 1920 (the NBER peak is January). Another forecaster said on March 26, 1923, "probabilities are becoming apparent that the Prosperity Period may be over around the beginning of 1924." [10] Cox considered this forecast wrong. His date for the downturn was May 1923 (the same as the NBER peak). The forecast for the last half of 1923 was for the wrong direction.

Cox's only explanation of the criteria he used in deciding whether a given forecast was right, neutral, or wrong consisted of the following: "A service which, within a given period prior to a major turn, was either silent or predicted a continuation of the existing rate of activity is assumed to have done its clients neither good nor harm. It is treated as having misled its clients only when it predicted a change in the wrong direction." [11] With so little to go on, one cannot be sure of the exact meaning of the data in Chart I-2. Our experience with scoring later forecasts by different methods suggests that Cox's scores, like ours, have a considerable element of subjectivity.

Panel B of Chart I-2 shows that, taking all eight peaks and troughs together, the percentage of correct predictions of the changed direction rises from 33 per cent six months before the cyclical reversal to 79 per cent three months after. Although it then falls off to 59 per cent and 53 per cent in the fourth and fifth months after the turning point, it rebounds to 71 per cent six months after the turn. The per cent of

scores were added and given a plus sign if the direction of change was correctly predicted, a minus sign if incorrectly predicted. Thus he derived a number representing the "adequacy" of each forecast. No use has been made here of his scores for amplitude and timing. Since the method underlying Chart I-2 utilizes only the correctness (or otherwise) of the forecasts of direction of change, omitting amplitude, the results may be biased in an upward direction. That is, a service that predicted the direction of change correctly gets full credit even if it thought the ensuing movement would be too minor to count, under NBER rules, as a cyclical expansion or contraction. Cox's scores cannot suitably be used here because, as he says, "In scoring a succession of forecasts, . . . the later the date of prediction of a turn the more definite it must be concerning time and amplitude in order to receive a given rating." (*Ibid.*, p. 34.) His numerical scores, therefore, do not exhibit the pattern of increasing recognition, since his method tends to eliminate the very increase we are interested in studying.

[9] Charles O. Hardy and Garfield V. Cox, *Forecasting Business Conditions,* New York, 1927, p. 348.

[10] *Ibid.,* p. 370.

[11] *American Business Forecasts,* 1st ed., pp. 30–31. This implies a neutral (zero) score if the forecaster predicted leveling off instead of a peak or trough. Presumably the "given period" begins with the first month in which any of the services correctly anticipated the coming turn.

wrong forecasts (not shown on the chart) fluctuates erratically between 5 and 14 per cent from six months before until two months after the turn. It then drops off to zero for two months.

In a broad way, the pattern shown in Chart I-2 is typical of what we shall find for more recent times. During the six months before a peak or trough, the percentage of services anticipating a change of direction is rather low. But it rises steadily, reaching its height a few months after the turn. In some respects, however, the results of the Cox-Moore analysis are surprising. The unexpectedly high percentage of correct anticipations before the turn may be attributed in part to the bias discussed in note 8. On the other hand, the maximum—79 per cent for all eight peaks and troughs, reached three months later—is considerably short of unanimity. Rather puzzling is the drop after plus three months instead of the rise that might have been expected. With some exceptions scores tend to be higher in the vicinity of troughs than at peaks (Panel A). Results similar in kind but more marked in degree will be presented below for 1948–61.

Cox's scores for correctness, on a scale from plus one to minus one, were designed for forecasts made at any time, not just in the vicinity of turning points.[12] A forecast made on February 13, 1919, that "this is bound to be a dull year in trade and transportation," for instance, was given the minimum score of minus one.[13] The year in fact was one of inflationary boom. A forecast made on October 11, 1923, that "the first half or three-quarters of 1924 is to be a time of trade reaction or mild depression, but not of anything worse," received the maximum score of plus one.[14] Zero was given for the statement made on November 18, 1926, that "the first half or two thirds of next year is likely to be a time of mild trade reaction" because Cox considered the prediction right with respect to what would happen but wrong as to timing.[15] In all his scoring, Cox's criterion was "whether the shaping of policy in

---

[12] Cox also scored the forecasts for definiteness on a scale of plus one to zero and multiplied the scores for definiteness and correctness to get a score for adequacy. These scores are not used here because, like the scores for timing, "a higher standard of definiteness was required concerning the *character,* of the predicted event if the service had indicated that it should be expected almost at once than if it had been thought to lie six months in the future." (*Ibid.,* p. 19.)

[13] *Ibid.,* pp. 17–18.

[14] *Ibid.,* p. 17.

[15] *Ibid.,* p. 18. Note that his peak date was March 1927. On the basis of the NBER peak of October 1926, this statement could be regarded as substantially correct.

conformity with the forecast in question would, on the whole, have been a step in the right direction or in the wrong one." [16] Predictions were assumed to apply to no more than eight months into the future unless the forecaster indicated otherwise. A forecast of conditions in a special sector was judged only by events in that sector. Forecasts of general business were checked either against the composite index of business activity specified by the service or, failing that, against three composite indexes (those of the Annalist, A.T.&T., and the Federal Reserve Bank of New York).

The relation of Cox's scores to recognition of cyclical turning points is not clear. The scores during the six months before and after a cyclical peak or trough may or may not pertain to forecasts of the turning points in question. Nevertheless, Chart I-3 is presented to supplement Chart I-2. It displays some tendency toward increasing correctness of forecasts as turns are approached and passed, but the tendency is less marked for the averages than in Chart I-2. For 1929, the scores fluctuate from month to month in a highly erratic fashion.

4

1948–61: Accuracy of Dating

For each of the eight turning points between 1948 and 1961, we have studied reports published by a number of contemporary observers. Like Cox, we first excerpted short quotations from current forecasts. We scored the excerpts in two different ways, for accuracy of dating and for degree of recognition. The scores for dating range from 0 to 100. The maximum score was given for designating a peak or trough within one month of the NBER date. A forecast that missed by two months received a score of 75; by three months, 50; by four months, 25. Thus, positive scores were given for forecasts of a peak or trough anywhere within a nine-month interval centered on the NBER reference date. A

[16] *Ibid.,* p. 19.

CHART I-4

Accuracy of Dating Cyclical Peaks and Troughs, Ten Analysts, 1948–61

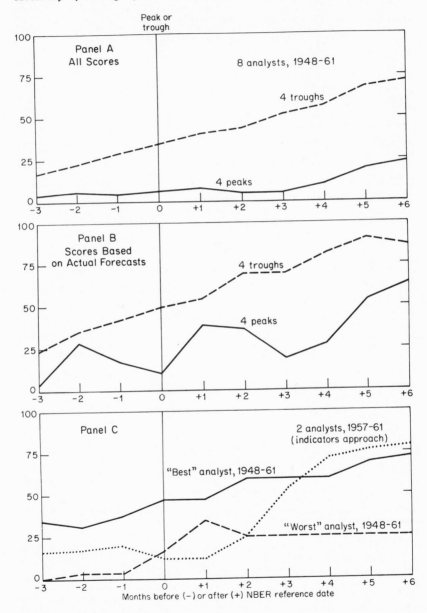

SOURCE: Appendix I, Table B.

of the turn had been made. (In 10 per cent of the cases, a score of zero was given because the forecast of the date was poor.) The remaining 13 per cent of the scores are positive scores carried forward from an earlier month. These figures, as indicated, include the two publications not available for all turns. These two made forecasts of dating more frequently than the others. For the eight alone, only 33 per cent of the scores are based on actual forecasts.

Panel B of Chart I-4 shows the results of excluding from the averages all of the zero scores based on no forecasts and a majority of the positive scores based on no forecasts. In a few cases, a positive score was retained because the publication clearly had no reason to repeat a conclusion already reached. Many of these cases occurred in 1961, when most forecasters knew within a few months that the trough had occurred in February, lost interest in the matter, and went on to discuss how vigorous the upswing would be. Positive scores not based on an actual forecast were retained only if three conditions were met: (1) the score was for a date no earlier than the second month after the NBER peak or trough; (2) the date given was not subsequently revised by the publication during the scoring period (i.e., within six months of the turn); (3) the accompanying certainty score (see the next chapter) was at least 75. If these three conditions were not met, failure to repeat an earlier forecast might have resulted from a change of opinion.

Since most of the scores thus excluded were zeros, the patterns in Panel B are higher than those in Panel A. The scores continue to be higher at troughs than at peaks. Panel B presumably overstates the ability of the eight publications to forecast the dates of turns, since failure to forecast a date can result from inability to do so. A fair assessment of forecasting ability probably lies somewhere between the patterns of the two panels. The data going into Panel A, however, have the advantage of greater comparability: for every month of every scoring period there are eight observations. The data for Panel B include a number of observations for each month varying from zero to eight.[20]

[20] The variation in number of observations means that a choice had to be made between two weighting systems in calculating the averages shown in Chart I-4, Panel B (the data for these can be found in Appendix I, Table B). Giving equal weight to each published forecast gives an upward bias, since more analysts give forecasts of dating in easy cases like 1961 (when only 8 per cent of the scores were excluded under our rules) than at turns hard to forecast like 1948 (when 89 per cent of the scores had to be dropped). The alternative of weighting each month equally regardless of the number of scores entering into that month's

For the sake of comparability, the dating scores discussed in the remainder of this paper include all scores whether based on forecasts or not.

There was a wide variation among the scores for individual analysts. For each analyst all the scores for the full ten-month period and for all eight turns were averaged. The averages ranged from 16 to 52. The median of the average scores of the eight analysts was 23, the mean 26. Panel C of Chart I-4 contrasts the patterns of the "best" and "worst" analysts. It also shows the average pattern for 1957–61 for the two publications that relied heavily on business cycle indicators.

A word of caution is in order about the "best" and the "worst" forecaster in Chart I-4, in other charts in my study, and in Hinshaw's comparison of the "best" with the Federal Open Market Committee. The "worst" analyst is the one with the lowest average score for degree of certainty (see the next chapter) but is only the second lowest with respect to accuracy of dating. The "best" analyst has the highest average score for both accuracy of dating and degree of certainty, taking peaks and troughs together. It has the highest scores, moreover, for peaks alone with respect to dating and for troughs alone with respect to both dating and certainty, but not for peaks alone with respect to certainty. In fact, its certainty scores at peaks were erratic—it had the highest score at one peak, the fourth highest at another peak, and the seventh highest (i.e., second worst) at the other two.[21] As a result, the so-called "best" displayed the greatest variability in certainty scores of the eight forecasters, even when all peaks and troughs are taken together. Since consistency is a virtue in forecasting, these considerations throw serious doubt as to whether the "best" can be considered a superior forecaster. Even its superiority with respect to dating is open to question on grounds that its higher scores resulted from the others ignoring the question of determining the date of the peak or trough. Of course, the range (or the uppermost observation) is in any event of limited value, since the range depends on the size of the sample. The best in a sample of eight is likely to be inferior to the best in a sample of eighty but superior to the best in a sample of four.

average (unless the number was zero) was therefore used instead. (A chart comparing the two procedures shows that the results are closely similar at troughs. At peaks the expected bias is evident but not great.)

[21] See Appendix I, Table J.

5

1948–61: Degree of Certainty

The quotations excerpted from the publications of the various analysts were scored for degree of certainty as well as for accuracy of dating. The user of forecasts needs to know not only what the forecast is but also the degree of confidence the forecaster has in it. Unfortunately, commentators often take refuge in ambiguity instead of giving odds on various precisely defined possibilities.

A general practice of communicating the degree of confidence in a forecast by stating subjective odds would not only be a clearer way of describing the outlook to the reader but would also facilitate retrospective appraisal of the record of predictions. For the specific purposes of the present study, increasing recognition of an imminent or recent peak would be revealed by rising odds on a downturn, and increasing recognition of a trough by rising odds on an upturn.[22]

The scoring system chosen was based on the odds on a cyclical turn implicit in the language of the forecast. Each quotation was scored for degree of recognition on a scale from 0 to 100 (since we only used multiples of five, there were twenty-one possible scores). A score of 50 means a roughly even chance of a cyclical turning point. A score of 100 represents virtual certainty (strictly speaking, chances greater than 97½ per cent).[23] As indicated earlier, each quotation was scored indepen-

[22] If all forecasters gave odds, in time a large enough sample would be generated to make possible a test of the hypothesis that half of the forecasts stated to have five chances in ten come true, 60 per cent of those given six chances in ten, etc. Such data, however, are too rare to make such a test.

[23] No corresponding statement can be made about low scores, which are biased downward compared to the implicit odds on a turning point. In the absence of any evidence to the contrary, we assumed that a publication regarded the odds of a turn in the target period as "normal." The target period is a three-month interval centered on the NBER reference date. Since recent expansions have averaged between two and three years in length (somewhat less in earlier times), the "normal" odds of a peak in any three-month interval during a period known to be an expansion may be taken as one in ten or a little less. Accordingly, we gave a publication a score of 10 in the vicinity of peaks unless it implied that

dently by C. Elton Hinshaw and myself, and discrepancies were resolved
by discussion as much as possible. When a doubt remained, the two
original scores were averaged.[24] The resulting scores are subjective.
Although in a majority of cases the two initial (independent) scores
were close together, in a disconcerting number of cases they differed
widely. The same person scoring the same series of forecasts after a
lapse of several months sometimes gave quite different scores.

As a result of both the nature of the materials and the procedures
followed, the scores are more reliable for tracing the pattern of
increasing recognition by a single forecaster than for comparing the
forecasts of different publications. Quite subtle shifts in wording and
emphasis from one month to the next by a given publication often
revealed fine shades of increasing uncertainty about prospects for continued expansion in the vicinity of peaks (and similarly for troughs);
this is why as many as twenty-one different possible scores were needed.
Even so, the scores could not always reflect discernible changes in the
attitudes of the forecasters. On the other hand, the difference in language
of different publications was often hard to interpret. It was much easier
to tell whether a given forecaster had become more or less optimistic
since last month than to tell whether he was more or less optimistic
than his fellows. Such difficulties, however, are minimal in the vicinity
of 50 and 100. If a forecaster expresses great certainty, the only question
is whether the score should be 95 or 100. Similarly, it is comparatively
easy to tell whether a forecaster thinks a turn more (or less) likely
than not. Therefore, errors in scoring on the wrong side of 50 are unlikely. This is fortunate because 50 can be regarded as the dividing
line between recognition and failure to recognize.

Our procedure was to score the ten (or more) quotations for a given
forecaster in succession before scoring other forecasters for the same
peak or trough. This procedure accentuated the inherent tendency for the
pattern of scores for a given forecaster to be more reliable than comparisons among different forecasters. Despite the weaknesses of the
scores, they are reliable enough for the purposes to which they are put

the odds were greater or less than "normal." Since contractions average shorter
than expansions, in the case of troughs we gave a score of 15 unless the publication implied that the odds were greater or less than normal. Defining the target
period as three months, however, turned out to be too restrictive and was not
adhered to rigidly for scores of 50 and higher.

[24] In the case of weekly publications, the weekly scores for each month were
averaged. Where we did not have quotations for a given week, we interpolated.

CHART I-5

Degree of Certainty of Forecasts of Cyclical Peaks and Troughs, Ten Analysts, 1948–61

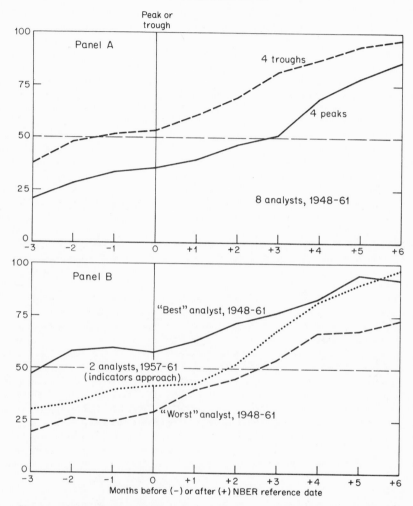

SOURCE: Appendix I, Table C.

here. But the reader should be cautioned against using the findings for more ambitious purposes.

Chart I-5 exhibits the expected pattern of increasing certainty over time. Panel A shows a marked difference between peaks and troughs.

CHART I-6

*Comparison of Scores for Accuracy of Dating at Four Peaks
and Four Troughs, 1948–61*
(averages of eight analysts)

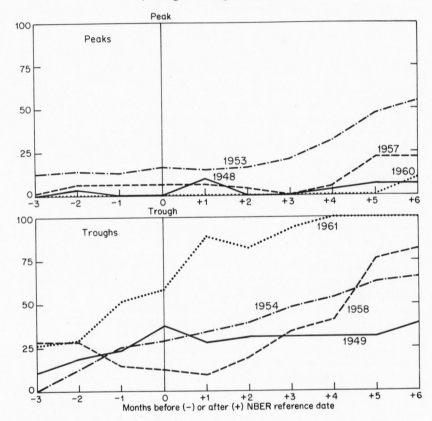

SOURCE: Appendix I, Table D.

At troughs, the mean score for eight forecasters first exceeds 50 (fifty-fifty odds) one month before the NBER reference date. At peaks, a mean of 50 is not achieved until three months after the reference dates. If confirmation is defined to mean an average score of 95 (95 per cent confidence), the group of analysts studied were able to confirm that a trough had occurred six months after the event but could not do so well for peaks. Averaging peaks and troughs together, only one of the ten analysts had an average score greater than 50 two months before the

CHART I-7

Comparison of Scores for Degree of Certainty at Four Peaks and Four Troughs, 1948–61
(averages of eight analysts)

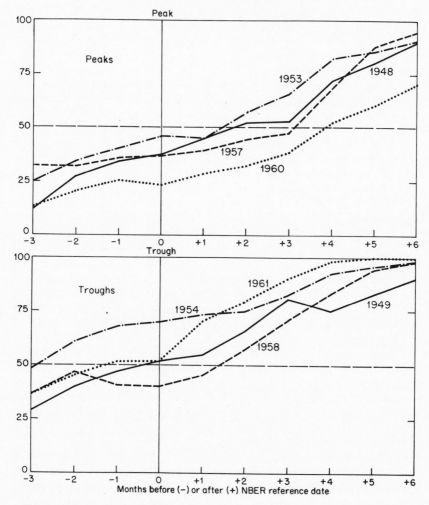

SOURCE: Appendix I, Table E.

reference date. Four out of eleven achieved an average score of 95 five months after the reference date (counting peaks and troughs together),[25] none earlier. If all scores for all months are averaged for each forecaster, the scores range from 44 to 71. The same publication that scored highest for timing also scored highest for degree of certainty. Panel B of Chart I-5 compares the "best" and the "worst" analysts for 1948–61. It also shows the average pattern for 1957–61 of the two publications that depended heavily on business cycle indicators.

All the average scores, for both accuracy of dating and degree of certainty, are subject to a serious limitation. As Charts I-6 and I-7 show, there is great variation among the scores for different turning points, not only the systematic differences between peaks and troughs already noted, but also differences among individual peaks and individual troughs. Discussion of each turn is in order.

6

The Recognition Pattern: A Chronological Review

The 1948 Peak

Scores for both dating and certainty run lower for peaks than for troughs, and among the four peaks since World War II, they run lower for 1948 than for any other year except 1960. Although there is nothing to choose between the certainty patterns for 1948 and 1957 shown in Chart I-7, the 1948 scores for dating are noticeably lower (see Chart I-6). Of the 80 scores for dating near the 1948 peak (eight forecasters, ten months), 75 were zero. (Seventy-one were zero because no forecast was made.)

---

[25] This includes one publication not used in the averages shown in Charts I-4 and I-5. The omission of this publication reduces the number with an average of 95 five months after the reference date to three in ten.

A reading of the quotations suggests that, although contemporary observers were prompt to recognize signs of cyclical weakness, they were slow to realize that a cyclical recession had begun. At the peak of the reference cycle in November 1948, comments ranged from, "The cyclical outlook has become more weighted in the direction of recession sometime in 1949" to "The boom will probably continue." During December, January, and February, there was a slow drift toward more pessimistic comments. Not until four and a half months after the peak of the business cycle did any of the sources studied decide that a recession was under way. In April, recession talk became more definite, but doubts persisted. Something like unanimity was reached only in May. It should be noted that the NBER method of dating peaks and troughs gives preference to the later of two equal months. In this case, October 1948 was a close runner-up to November for reference cycle peak. Historically, contractions have sometimes been as short as seven or eight months, and under the NBER definition of business cycles, a contraction might be even shorter. Even with allowance for the information lag, there was enough data by the end of June to establish that the contraction was a historical fact without any element of prediction. All in all, recognition of the 1948 peak hardly constituted a triumph for the art of forecasting.

Low scores for dating and certainty, however, do not of themselves prove that the performance of business analysts was poor. Some contractions start so slowly, as in 1960, that they are inherently difficult to distinguish from lulls until four or five months after the peak. But the turn of 1948 was not of that sort. Information that could have been available three months after the peak was more clear-cut and decisive than for most peaks and troughs since World War II.[26]

Why, then, did contemporary observers have so much trouble recognizing what was going on? Statistical reporting and analysis were not so highly developed then as now. The postwar work on business cycle indicators by Moore, Shiskin, and others had not been published. But the 1948 recognition record does not look good even in comparison with the earlier case of 1929. There must be some more basic explanation.

[26] Compare the charts for three months after each peak and trough of Julius Shiskin, *Signals of Recession and Recovery, An Experiment with Monthly Reporting,* Occasional Paper 77, New York: National Bureau of Economic Research, 1961, pp. 93–99 (see also pp. 57–58 and 100–105). Cf. Chart I-1 of this paper, especially the leads of some of the series.

When conditions change violently, the forecaster is at a disadvantage. He cannot tell to what extent his past knowledge is still valid. The later 1940's followed a decade and a half of unusually rapid change in American economic life. The experience of living through a depression of unprecedented depth changed people's conduct. The structure of the economic system had been transformed, and the war had altered economic variables in ways that had only distant parallels with the previous world war. At first, forecasters did not realize how much more difficult their problem had become, and they plunged confidently ahead with predictions. But the widely publicized forecasts of severe depression to follow World War II turned out to be ingloriously wrong. Those forecasters who in 1945 had assumed that the consumption function of the 1930's would still hold good came to grief, as did those who assumed that chronic stagnation of investment would reassert itself. So too did those who thought in terms of primary and secondary postwar depressions. Later, in 1947, a decline in industrial production was widely misinterpreted as the beginning of recession. Instead, it was followed by another bout of inflation. Again, in early 1948, a break in farm prices raised the question of recession prematurely. By the time the downturn actually came, commentators and forecasters had learned to be cautious. Their uncertainty was reinforced by the President, who continued to advocate an anti-inflationary program. But slow recognition was more than just a matter of caution born of experience. Analysts faced a genuinely difficult problem. The inflation that followed the 7 per cent drop in the index of industrial production in 1947 (a drop that was largely obliterated as a result of the 1953 revision of the seasonal adjustment) gave them ample reason to wonder if the comparatively small decline in the winter of 1949 might not have a similar sequel. Knowledge that government expenditures were to rise sharply worked in the same direction. The structural changes in the economy raised the question of whether the business cycle was a thing of the past. And finally, the experience of 1929–48 had led observers to think in terms of deep depression and rapid inflation, not of business cycles with the mild contractions that have characterized postwar experience.

The 1949 Trough

Among troughs, the scores for 1949 are lowest, though the difference from 1958 is slight. (To be precise, the averages of the certainty scores for the two years are virtually the same, with the average for dating somewhat higher for 1958.) The scores might have been even lower for 1949, especially the certainty scores, had the trough not been double-bottomed.[27] The first bottom came in July. The expansion that ensued was soon interrupted by strikes in coal and steel. The second bottom, in October, is the one designated by the NBER as the reference cycle trough.

Contemporary observers were quick to note the end of cyclical contraction but slow to predict cyclical expansion. Although in July some commentators were expecting further contraction, others noted signs of recovery. In the next two or three months there was a gradual increase in optimism tempered by fears the recovery would be short-lived. In November, as the country began recovering from the strikes, the comments on the outlook either were ambiguous or portended a sidewise movement. In December the typical view was optimistic about the first half of 1950 and doubtful about the second half. In January, a future chairman of the Council of Economic Advisers, though expecting business to improve over the next few months, felt the contemporary CEA's conclusion that the economy was definitely recovering from the contraction was "based on very slight evidence." During the next few months, the general pessimism about the second half of 1950 gave way to optimism.

In the neighborhood of the 1948 peak, contemporary observers did not seem to be thinking in business cycle terms. The same is true of 1949–50. In 1949, observers were rather quicker than in 1948 to perceive what had just happened, but they were slower to draw inferences of a cyclical nature. In fact, so far as I have been able to discover, none of the publications in my sample used cyclical language.

The 1953 Peak

Among peaks, the highest scores for both timing and recognition were given for 1953, as Charts I-6 and I-7 indicate, even though these

[27] The effect of the double bottom on dating scores was mixed, since one of the publications dated the trough in July and suffered lower scores accordingly, perhaps undeservedly. But the belief that the "true" trough had been in July made for greater certainty that expansion was under way once the October strikes were over, a circumstance reinforcing the purely mechanical effects that a later reference date has in raising certainty scores by shifting forward the ten-month period used for scoring purposes.

scores run lower than for any trough. The NBER has dated the 1953 peak in July, a decision that has not been challenged. A number of sources gave early warning. In June every member of a group of forecasters studied by Zarnowitz predicted that industrial production would decline in the second half of the year. Moreover, the amplitude of the mean of their forecasts approximated what actually happened. In July comments generally pointed downward though they were not unanimous. In August they were rather definite about expecting decline but indefinite or conflicting about whether the decline would constitute a cyclical contraction or recession. In September they were still indefinite. Insofar as recognition of the contraction increased in October, it revealed itself mainly in the expressed expectation that the decline would be mild. But at the end of the month, one source used the expression, "now that the decline has come. . . ." During November, most of the others made similar statements, though the language was often indirect or ambiguous.

Improvement in recognition over 1948 was marked. During the month of the peak, and even before, there was widespread knowledge, or at least fear, that business activity was about to head downward. From then on, however, the conviction that that was indeed what was happening strengthened slowly. Although, in terms of confirmation, they did scarcely any better than in 1948 in giving early warning, the sources studied, with few exceptions, did well.

Why the improvement? Between the peaks of 1948 and 1953, Geoffrey H. Moore, C. Ashley Wright, and Thor Hultgren had published results of their investigations of business cycle indicators.[28] One of the sources studied made direct use of Wright's analyses. There is evidence that the Council of Economic Advisers made use of the NBER indicators. Other publications on business cycles together with the experience of 1948–49 may have made observers more sensitive to cyclical downturns. But it is hard to believe that the growth of knowledge, which is slow, could account for more than part of the improvement.

The 1953 turning point was inherently easier to anticipate than the one in 1948. Although the inflation of 1946–48 was bound to come to

[28] Geoffrey H. Moore, *Statistical Indicators of Cyclical Revivals and Recessions,* New York, NBER Occasional Paper 31, 1950; C. Ashley Wright, "Business Cycle Research and Business Policy," *Conference on Business Cycles,* New York, NBER, 1951, pp. 339–368; Thor Hultgren, *Cyclical Diversities in the Fortunes of Industrial Corporations,* New York, NBER Occasional Paper 32, 1950.

an end as rising prices reduced the value of liquid assets, as rising civilian output alleviated the most pressing shortages, and as the proportion of disposable income saved returned to normal, nevertheless the time when inflationary pressures would subside was difficult to foretell; and diagnosis in November 1948 was made especially difficult by continuing shortages of automobiles, the tax cut of 1948, and the prospective rise in government expenditures. Moreover, there was no reason in 1948 to think inventories were out of line with output or sales. The Korean war, in contrast, left no legacy of shortages and accumulated liquid assets. The end of the war was easy to foresee, as was the lag of tax cuts behind the reduction of government expenditures. Before the peak, inventories built up unintentionally. That the Federal Reserve System had tightened credit too much was so obvious that it moved to relax credit even before the downturn. In 1953, unlike early 1949, no one questioned whether or not there would be another burst of inflation simply because there was no reason to raise the question. Consequently, the signals of impending cyclical contraction were easier to believe.

The 1954 Trough

The scores for degree of certainty in the vicinity of the 1954 trough average higher than for any other turn between 1948 and 1961; the scores for accuracy of dating were second highest. To some extent the seemingly good performance of the business analysts may be the result of a close decision on the date of the trough. The trough was flat-bottomed. In the successive revisions of GNP, its low has shifted from the second quarter of 1954 to the first, then to the third, back again to the first, and finally to the second. The FRB index of industrial production has twice had its trough relocated through revision. The NBER has dated the reference cycle trough in August. The date may get changed to May, June, or July when it is re-examined in the light of the latest statistics, although the troughs in the various series of employment and unemployment (inverted) came in July, August, and September. An earlier date for the reference trough would shift the pattern shown in Chart I-7 downward to the right and alter the relative standing of 1954. Dating the trough in May would make the certainty pattern the lowest of the four instead of the highest.

As early as May, or even earlier, some contemporary observers thought that the cyclical contraction was coming to an end. They correctly anticipated a prolonged period of bottoming out but underestimated the speed the recovery would attain thereafter. Although many observers continued to be indecisive about expansion (as distinct from the ending of contraction), more and more of them became definite during September, October, and November, and they were more inclined to think in business cycle terms than in 1949.

The 1957 Peak

Though the improvement in scores in 1953 over 1948 was partly the result of a situation inherently easier to diagnose, it seems also to reflect improvement in the ability of business analysts to recognize downturns. The scores fell off in 1957, and fell still further in 1960. Did the falling off result from a decline in ability to recognize peaks when they occur or from cyclical developments that were harder to assess?

The NBER dates the 1957 peak in July, a close choice over August. Many forecasters gave warning of a cyclical turn misleadingly early, well before the first month for which we have assigned scores. Though the initial scores for certainty averaged higher than at any other peak, warnings of recession were less frequent three months before the peak than they had been earlier and increased very slowly during the next several months. At the peak in July, commentators were universally aware that business had slowed down but, with certain exceptions to be discussed later, did not conclude that a recession was beginning. Many were noncommittal, others optimistic. There was a shift toward pessimism in August, September, and October, but the tenor of reports on the outlook was still indecisive. On October 30, President Eisenhower acknowledged publicly, "the economy is, in effect, taking a breather." After that, one might have expected recognition of the cyclical downturn to become universal quickly. Actually, though certainty scores for November spurted upward, there were at least two holdouts (scores of 35 and 50), with the lowest score going to the publication with the best over-all recognition record for 1948–61.

Why was the certainty record of the eight poorer in 1957 than in 1953? Testimony in early June of 1957 by a panel of forecasters before a Congressional committee is revealing. No member of the panel was expecting recession. Their testimony shows that they were misinformed about investment in inventories, investment in plant and equipment, and federal spending. Surveys misled them into thinking spending on plant and equipment would continue to rise slightly during the remainder of the year. The forecasters thought government spending was rising. One of them feared inflation. He thought net disinvestment in inventories was taking place during the current (second) quarter. He concluded that by the end of the year cessation of inventory liquidation would give demand a boost. Events turned out just the opposite. Instead of liquidation, there was net accumulation of inventories during the first three quarters of the year; decumulation instead of accumulation took place in the fourth. A sharp cut in defense procurement (which the panel could hardly have known was about to begin) and a downward slide of capital investment helped precipitate the recession.

Forecasters always have to work with inaccurate information. Usually some of the errors offset each other. In this case, they all worked in the same direction. Of the three errors, one was of decisive importance. In May the Department of Commerce had published an estimate for the first quarter showing a substantial negative figure for inventory investment, leading forecasters to think the economy had already weathered an inventory adjustment. Revised figures now show substantial positive inventory investment.

Failure to give clearer warning that a contraction might be under way was also associated with the persistence of inflation, in the form of rising consumer prices, after the cyclical peak was passed. The concern for fighting inflation, felt during the summer and early fall by prominent government officials including the President and the Federal Reserve Board (which raised discount rates in August), communicated itself to the public and permeated the background of all discussions of the outlook. Professional forecasters presumably were familiar with the fact that consumer prices lag behind wholesale prices. But the climate of opinion can influence them too.[29]

If the President's influence depressed certainty scores during the three months after the peak, it also contributed to their rapid rise in

[29] It can also affect what they are willing to say in print. If, as I suspect, most of the publications reviewed were sympathetic with Eisenhower's efforts to stop inflation, they might have been reluctant to embarrass him.

November. Seldom is it possible to pinpoint so definitely the time at which knowledge of a cyclical turning point became general. Prior to October 30, nearly everybody had hesitated to say definitely that there was a recession. After Eisenhower's "breather" remark and the reduction of discount rates by the Federal Reserve two weeks later, there was less hesitation. But most of the credit belongs to the Council of Economic Advisers (whose briefing led to the "breather" remark), to the statistical indicators they made use of,[30] and to the Federal Reserve Board.

The 1958 Trough

The scores for the 1958 trough were lower than those for 1954, especially with respect to certainty, and lower than those for 1961, especially with respect to dating. In late 1957, almost as soon as the existence of recession became confirmed, a number of forecasters predicted that it would be brief and mild. In a loose and vague way, therefore, they gave early warning of the trough of April 1958. But the actual upturn came sooner than expected. When it came, commentators were reasonably prompt to confirm it.

At the end of February, a prominent economist thought there was "real danger . . . of a cumulative breakdown in the economy." During the trough month of April, there was general recognition that the contraction was slowing down but little realization that it was about to give way to expansion. Comments in May resembled those of April, yet conveyed an air of greater hopefulness. By the middle of June, improvement was widely recognized, but views diverged as to whether it would continue. Five out of the ten certainty scores were less than 50. Only one of the sources studied said flatly, "the upturn is now a fact and not just an expectation." July brought many converts to the view that expansion was under way, though none put it as unqualifiedly as the passage just quoted. Only one score was now below 50. In August the remainder of the sources studied became converted. The lowest score was 65, with two scores of 100.

[30] In the fall of 1957, the chairman of the Council of Economic Advisers asked the Census Bureau to develop a monthly report on indicators. The request led eventually to publication of *Business Cycle Developments*. (Julius Shiskin, *Signals of Recession and Recovery: An Experiment with Monthly Reporting,* New York, NBER Occasional Paper 77, 1961, p. 1.)

The 1960 Peak

The scores for both dating and certainty were lower in the vicinity of the 1960 peak than for any other turning point, peak or trough, of the eight between 1948 and 1961. Although all turning points are hard to predict, the 1960 reversal was harder than most.[31] A severe steel strike in 1959 interfered with interpretation of the business cycle indicators, many of which exhibited early peaks that were obviously spurious. When some of them again showed local peaks in the restocking period after the strike, the signals were neither unmistakable nor unambiguous.

A bulge in inventory investment was expected to give the economy a strong upward thrust in the first half of 1960. The aftermath of the restocking period was expected to be a decline in inventory investment with unfavorable repercussions on the economy as a whole. But forecasters drew the conclusion that the outcome would be a slower rate of expansion rather than an immediate downturn, with a strong possibility of a recession beginning late in 1960 or early in 1961. Their logic seems at fault. Their diagnoses implied that the danger point would come at midyear rather than at year's end.

Expectation of a continued advance in the second half of 1960 resulted from specific analysis of the forces at work, particularly from surveys showing that businesses were planning to increase spending on plant and equipment. Some forecasters also expected that inventory accumulation would continue, though at a reduced rate, in the second half of the year.[32]

The NBER has designated May as the reference cycle peak. The date

[31] These statements are subject to an important qualification. Two economists as early as the spring of 1959 were expecting a downturn in the spring of 1960, and a third warned Vice President Nixon in February 1960 of the danger. The predictions of all three were strongly influenced by the tight money policy of the Federal Reserve System.

[32] The forecast of continued expansion throughout 1960 was not unreasonable. The upper turning point was so flat and the ensuing contraction was so mild that, one may infer, absence of any of the deflationary forces actually at work would have prevented the cyclical turn. One of the factors at work was the failure of consumer spending to rise in the third quarter in spite of a rise in disposable personal income. This development and its consequences could hardly have been predicted with the forecasting tools available in 1960 (or now, for that matter). Nevertheless, the forecasters ought to have been able to give clearer warning to the effect that, though the outlook was favorable, the odds in favor of recession were by no means negligible. (I am indebted to Dennis R. Starleaf's unpublished study of the 1960 turn in this connection.)

is reasonable, although a critic has proposed July as a possible alternative.[33] A July date would make the certainty pattern shown in
Chart I-7 look better but not especially good. Even among minor cycles,
the contraction of 1960–61 was unusually short and mild. As might be
expected from these characteristics, the turn was flat rather than sharp,
making it intrinsically hard to recognize.

At the beginning of 1960, as already noted, the standard forecast
called for vigorous expansion in the first half of the year. As early as
February, there were expressions of mild disappointment. "High plateau"
was the common expression in March. In the following month comments
were, on the whole, indecisive. During May, the peak month, comments
ranged from considerable optimism through mild optimism to dubious-
ness. During the next three months, there were numerous revisions of
views, some in one direction, some in the other. On balance there was
some shift toward pessimism, but the eight publications for which scores
are available from 1948 on did not achieve an average score greater
than 50 for certainty till September. Despite the difficulties of recognizing a flat turning point, it is surprising that recognition did not become
general during October. To what extent the political campaign inhibited
facing facts is hard to say. Not until election day could recognition of
the contraction be considered general, and then only on the assumption
that some sources knew more than they had put into print.

The 1961 Trough

The turn for which scores ran lowest was followed by the one for which
they ran highest. The scores for degree of certainty in the vicinity of
the 1961 trough, though good, averaged lower than in 1954, but the
dating scores were much higher (see Charts I-6 and I-7).

The circumstances that made recognition of the 1960 peak difficult
helped make recognition of the 1961 trough easy. The flat top of the
1960 peak and the mildness of the ensuing contraction made it difficult
to know whether there was a contraction at all but made it natural to
expect that, if there were one, it would end soon. Moreover, the 1960–
61 contraction was something of an accident. In a situation basically

[33] In the latest revision of the national income accounts, the peak in GNP
in constant dollars comes in the first quarter, making a date for the reference
cycle peak as late as July implausible. (*Survey of Current Business,* August 1965,
p. 27.) The quarter-to-quarter variations, however, are so slight that little confidence can be put in the estimate of where the peak in real GNP belongs.

favorable to continued expansion, exogenous disturbances barely sufficed to set in motion the mechanism of inventory contraction. The contraction could not get very far in the face of automatic stabilizers, reversal of monetary policy, increasing net exports, and an early rise in defense orders. The basically favorable situation made it easy to anticipate an early upturn. The trough, however, came sooner than most observers expected; hence, the dating scores shown in Chart I-6 were not especially high until one month before the trough.

The favorable circumstances resulted in a sharp upturn, helping to make the trough easy to date and recognize. The bottom started like a U and ended like a V. Since, under NBER procedures, the later date is preferred in doubtful cases, a trough that is half U and half V, in that order, does not give rise to difficulties. The NBER reference date of February has not been challenged.

In November and December, almost as soon as the various commentators declared a recession was under way, they predicted that it would be short and mild. In January the most common expectation was still for a mild recession, with an upturn by midyear. During the month of the cyclical trough, there was, with some exceptions, a tendency to advance the date of the expected upturn. In March, with varying degrees of certainty, all the sources surveyed expressed the view that the upturn was at hand or, at the least, not far off. During April, they became more certain, week by week. During the first part of May, lingering doubts about the reality of the upturn tended to disappear. The question shifted to how fast recovery was proceeding. The answer given was that it was proceeding more rapidly than most observers had expected.

7

False Warnings

False warnings may be considered reverse recognition. This chapter examines some of the most flagrant cases. Our method of scoring for accuracy of dating cannot, of course, be readily adapted to false warn-

ings. The scoring for degree of certainty could be adapted to false warnings more easily, though we have not attempted to do so.[34] But false
warnings should be considered because a forecasting record must be
discounted if it achieves success at turns that do occur only by ignoring
the hazard of false warnings.

The head of a forecasting service has been quoted as having said early
in 1931, "Statistics show clearly that business reached its low point in
December of last year. Since then there has been a steady but constant
improvement. Everything indicates that general business has turned the
corner. . . . I go further and say that 1931 should offer the greatest
opportunities of any year for generations."

In May 1947, in separate statements, two professors from the same
university used almost identical language, one saying, "The long expected and long advertised recession is here," the other saying, "Beyond
question, the long advertised recession is here." A month later in a news
magazine with a large circulation was the statement, "The nation's
bumper crop of economic forecasters could now relax, tuck their
thumbs in their vest, and say: 'We told you so.' The recession had of-
ficially begun." The basis for that confident assertion was the index of
industrial production. The index was revised in 1953 in a way that
eliminated most of the decline.[35] The mean of the forecasts of industrial
production made in September by a group of forecasters in Zarnowitz'
collection predicted a decline from a high in the first half of the year,
the decline to continue for the year and a half covered by the prediction
and to aggregate more than 10 per cent—clearly an amplitude of
cyclical proportions. What is worse, every single forecaster in the group
predicted a decline in industrial production. The top of the range of
forecasts predicted the same level of industrial production for the second
half of 1947 as for the first half, with the first half of 1948 3 per cent

[34] See, however, p. xvi above.
[35] *Federal Reserve Bulletin,* December 1953, pp. 1239–1291. The extent of
the decline from March through July 1947 was reduced from 7 per cent to 2 per
cent, mainly because of a change in the seasonal adjustment. This is a very
interesting example of the difficulties inherent in recognizing the current cyclical
position. The "correct" seasonal adjustment cannot be known until data for
future years become available. In this particular case, the difficulty was magnified
because 1947 was the first year in which the normal postwar seasonal pattern
became manifest. Hindsight makes clear what could not be clear to contemporary
observers: the fall in industrial production was mainly seasonal in character.

lower and the second half slightly lower still. True, not everybody in the group expected a decline of cyclical proportions.

Though the NBER does not consider 1951–52 a business cycle contraction, it is a borderline case. At the same time that defense spending in connection with the Korean war gave one part of the economy an inflationary thrust, the civilian sector underwent a decline in demand as well as in output. Inventory investment fell from $15 billion in 1950-IV and 1951-II (about 5 per cent of GNP) to a negative figure in 1952-II, a decline greater than that associated with most so-called inventory recessions. GNP itself did not fall, though it leveled off temporarily.[36] Under such circumstances, one might expect to find some forecasters giving false warnings. One business publication in the summer of 1951 said, "Business in general is undergoing a minor recession and many businessmen are facing a downright slump. . . ." It went on to say that its projections "suggest a 'deflationary' not an 'inflationary' gap between the first quarter of 1951 and the first quarter of 1952." In the spring of 1952, another publication said that if a steel strike came, "we think it would add something to the prospects for second half year general revival in business, since it would deepen the current recession by taking a key industry out of production." In mitigation of these offenses, it should be pointed out that the term "minor recession" or even just plain "recession" as used by the publications under review does not have as precise a meaning as it does when used by economists.[37]

Another difficult time for forecasters came in 1956. GNP in constant dollars fell from $446.4 in 1955-IV to $443.6 in 1956-I and from $445.6 in 1956-II to $444.5 in 1956-III.[38] One forecaster relying primarily on business cycle indicators in May 1956 was rather sure a cyclical peak had occurred in February. A business publication that in January had forecast a $5 billion decline (more than 1 per cent) in the

---

[36] More precisely, the most recent estimates show a decline in GNP in current dollars of one-tenth of 1 per cent in 1952-II, a decline in GNP in constant dollars of one-half of 1 per cent. In 1952-III, GNP resumed its rise.

[37] That the forecasters' use of "recession" does not necessarily imply a business cycle contraction came as an unhappy surprise to me, making the task of interpreting and scoring forecasts more difficult. Moreover, the word may be used at different times by the same publication in different senses. This is a specific example of a general tendency by forecasters to take refuge in ambiguity.

[38] These are the most recent estimates from *Survey of Current Business*, August 1965, pp. 26–27. Earlier estimates told a roughly similar story. GNP in current dollars continued to rise (*ibid.*, pp. 24–25). Figures in the text are in billions.

rate of GNP during 1956 said in its July issue, "To be sure, a business 'recession' has been under way since the end of 1955. But . . . it's a 'friendly' recession. That is to say, industrial production has eased only two per cent since last December and the nation's total output of goods and services has continued to rise. Thus the current business readjustment has been much less severe, for example, than the readjustment of 1949 or 1953–54. . . ." The passage just quoted abounds in ambiguity.[39]

As a business publication later said, 1962 "was a year when many forecasters broke their crystal balls in agonized frustration." A government economist said at the time, "As soon as consumer confidence is shaken, and the consumer limits his spending, the effects can be seen through the whole industrial economy—and I think the process has already started." During a thirteen month period, one of the publications in our sample was continuously forecasting a peak with such a high degree of confidence that, under our methods of scoring for degree of certainty, it would have been given scores ranging from 80 to 100 had a peak actually occurred.

Although I have called the forecasts reviewed in this section "false warnings" or "false alarms" and have even referred to them as "flagrant cases," in a sense they were not false alarms at all. In all of the periods in question—1931, 1947, 1951–52, 1956, and 1962—the economy actually did hesitate and show signs of reversing itself. Such hesitations are hard to distinguish contemporaneously from turning points. Some economists believe that they should be recognized as a separate class of phenomena in addition to the usual cyclical phases of expansion and contraction.

---

[39] The publication in question was the same one that in 1951 had said the economy was "undergoing a minor recession." In January 1958, in the course of denying that the economy was then experiencing "a real 'recession,'" it said, "time was when 'recession' was reserved for an industrial decline of 15 per cent or more, usually accompanied by slumps of one-third or more in capital spending." Unfortunately, this publication has not issued a glossary defining the differences among "minor recession," "'friendly' recession," and "real 'recession.'"

8

Recognition Methods

It is hard to get evidence on the comparative success of different methods of recognizing cyclical turns, because all analysts are to some extent eclectic. Two main methods, however, can be distinguished in principle and sometimes in practice as well. Perhaps the most popular method of forecasting uses the national income framework. Separate provisional forecasts are made for the components of GNP. These are added and revised in the light of any discrepancies between the total and the assumptions underlying the provisional forecasts. Such a forecast may yield a prediction of a turning point, especially if it is a quarterly multiperiod forecast.[40] The other principal method uses the business cycle indicators. Besides these two well-recognized methods, the quantity theory of money can be and sometimes is used as a basis for forecasting turning points. And it is possible to forecast without any recognizable method at all other than interpretation of available data with the help of theory, experience, judgment, and intuition.

Since the discussions of turning points by the eight analysts in our main group were mostly informal, I cannot tell to what extent they relied on national income models, on the indicators, or on something else. For want of more knowledge and a better name, I shall refer to them as "eclectic." Two other publications, available for only part of the period under study here, relied heavily on business cycle indicators. In addition, Victor Zarnowitz has generously furnished me with data based on multiperiod forecasts of GNP (mostly quarterly). There is a presumption that Zarnowitz' forecasters relied more heavily on national income models than the two in my sample who used the indicators.

---

[40] The econometric method may be regarded in principle as a variant of this method, since econometric forecasts commonly use the national income framework. Because data for assessing the recognition record of the econometric method is meager, I shall not discuss it further. The accuracy of econometric forecasts is, however, being studied by Jon Cunnyngham as a part of the National Bureau's project.

Data for both users of the indicators approach can be had for only four turns (1957–61). Comparison of the average scores of these two with the eight eclectics for the four turns together conceals such diversity that its value is doubtful.[41] Suffice it to say that the comparison does not establish any striking differences in the success of the two groups.

Although the average scores of the two and the eight do not display marked differences for the four turns between 1957 and 1961 taken together, the same is not true for individual turns. In 1957 (see Chart I-8), the two using the indicators approach scored better on degree of certainty than the other eight in nine out of the ten months scored, and during the early months the difference was marked.[42] The inaccurate statistical information on inventory investment in 1957 affected users of national income analysis more than those who put their faith in business cycle indicators.[43]

Whereas the two relying heavily on the indicators scored better with respect to degree of certainty than the eight in 1957, the following year it was the other way round (see Chart I-9). In this case, a scrap of addi-

[41] The two users of indicators had average scores for accuracy of dating a shade higher than the average of the eight eclectics during the three months before the four turns (between 1957 and 1961). Their forecasts of dating were markedly worse at and immediately after the turn, but during the period from three to six months after the reference dates, their scores for accuracy of dating were considerably higher. These results give no evidence that the indicators are especially helpful in determining dating contemporaneously with cyclical turns. The suggestion that the indicators have considerable value some months after the turn is subject to the qualification that many of the other analysts lacked interest in the question of dating. They were concerned with whether a peak or trough had occurred; exactly when it occurred did not matter. The very decision to use the indicators may imply a greater interest in the subject.

The publications relying on the indicators had average scores for degree of certainty slightly higher than the eight eclectics, but not enough higher, in view of the shortcomings of the scoring procedures, to warrant anything in the way of conclusions about recognition methods (except, perhaps, the speculation that recognition depends more on the judgment of the analyst than on the specific methods he uses).

[42] Both groups did poorly with respect to accuracy of dating in 1957. Which did worse depends on whether the mean or the median is used for the eight, the median being zero in every single month. One of the two users of indicators had poor scores (mostly zeroes) because he consistently dated the peak much too early. The other one first predicted a date much too late and thereafter ignored the subject.

[43] Although inventory investment is now one of the NBER leading indicators, it was not put on the list until 1960 (Moore, *Business Cycle Indicators,* Vol. I, p. 55). What is more to the point, the indicator approach, which uses a substantial number of series without formally weighting them, is less likely to be affected by an error in any one series.

CHART I-8

Recognition Scores in the Vicinity of the 1957 Peak:
Comparison of Indicators Approach with Eclectic Approach

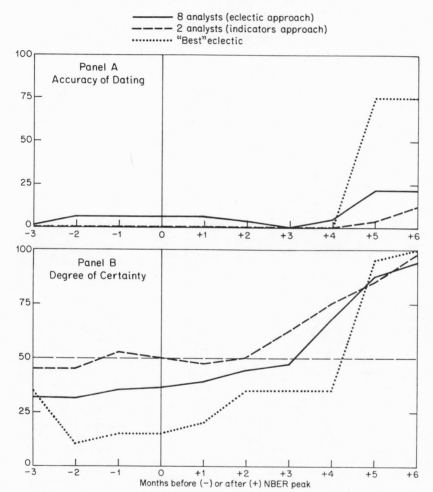

——— 8 analysts (eclectic approach)
– – – 2 analysts (indicators approach)
············ "Best" eclectic

Panel A
Accuracy of Dating

Panel B
Degree of Certainty

Months before (−) or after (+) NBER peak

SOURCE: Appendix I, Table F.

tional information tends to support the hypothesis that a difference in method was responsible. An economist's testimony before a Congressional committee at the end of April made it clear that (1) his prediction of a weak upturn in the third quarter was based on a GNP

CHART I-9

Recognition Scores in the Vicinity of the 1958 Trough:
Comparison of Indicators Approach with Eclectic Approach

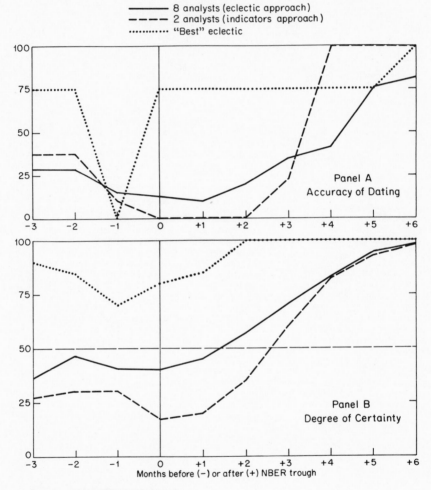

——— 8 analysts (eclectic approach)
– – – – 2 analysts (indicators approach)
·············· "Best" eclectic

Panel A
Accuracy of Dating

Panel B
Degree of Certainty

Months before (−) or after (+) NBER trough

SOURCE: Appendix I, Table G.

model and (2) his low confidence that the upturn would materialize
was based on the NBER indicators, which did not look good to him.

In 1960 (Chart I-10), those using the indicators again outscored the
other eight, this time in accuracy of dating as well as in degree of certainty. Although in February and March they succeeded no better than

CHART I-10

Recognition Scores in the Vicinity of the 1960 Peak:
Comparison of Indicators Approach with Eclectic Approach

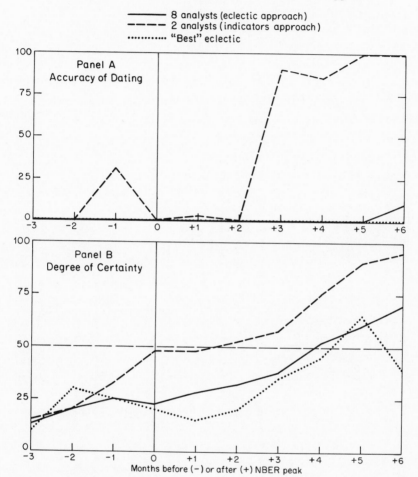

──────── 8 analysts (eclectic approach)
── ── ── 2 analysts (indicators approach)
·············· "Best" eclectic

Source: Appendix I, Table H.

the others in anticipating the turn, later on they were more alert to early signs that it was already past. But they did not do as well as the three other economists alluded to earlier in footnote 31, two of whom on the basis of Federal Reserve policy called the turn as early as the spring of 1959.

CHART I-11

Recognition Scores in the Vicinity of the 1961 Trough:
Comparison of Indicators Approach with Eclectic Approach

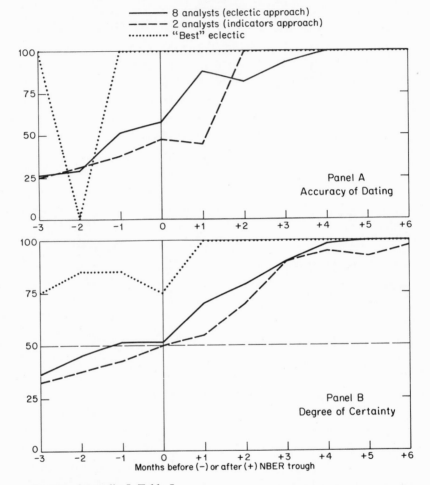

8 analysts (eclectic approach)
2 analysts (indicators approach)
"Best" eclectic

Panel A
Accuracy of Dating

Panel B
Degree of Certainty

Months before (−) or after (+) NBER trough

SOURCE: Appendix I, Table I.

In 1961 (Chart I-11), the eight eclectics outscored the two relying on indicators with respect to both accuracy and certainty.

In sum, if dubious evidence can be believed, the indicators seem quicker than eclectic methods to give warning of downturns and slower to herald upturns. The result may, however, reflect a difference in outlook. The eight eclectics in general scored higher at troughs than peaks, a result consistent with the hypothesis that they inclined toward optimism. (Reading the forecasts of the "best" of the eight gives a strong impression of an optimistic bias on its part. Compare Charts I-8 and I-10 with I-9 and I-11.) Those forecasters who decided to put their faith largely in business cycle indicators may have done so because by temperament and training they were inclined to think in terms of peaks and troughs. (Reading the forecasts of one of the two gives a strong impression of a watch for the next peak as soon as the trough is past.) The two may not have shared the optimistic outlook of the others.[44] But the two may not be representative of users of the indicators, and the eight may have used indicators more heavily than appears to have been the case. Firm conclusions cannot be reached about methods where individual judgment is as important as in forecasting.

Let us turn now to a comparison of Zarnowitz' sample with mine. Zarnowitz has provided data for four sets of forecasts (A, C, D, and G, as he designates them). Two of the sets represent company forecasts of GNP. The other two result from averaging the GNP forecasts of groups of economists who made their forecasts simultaneously and on a comparable basis. Altogether there are twenty-four forecasts made in the vicinity of actual cyclical turns, yielding thirty-six observations (since these are multiperiod forecasts, the same forecast may predict—or not predict—two actual turns occurring close together). In addition, there are six forecasts yielding seven observations of predicted turns that did not occur. Since the forecasts were made at rather infrequent intervals, it is not possible to trace the pattern of increasing recognition in Zarnowitz' sample nor to make a complete comparison with mine.

I scored the thirty-six observations pertaining to actual turns for both accuracy of timing and degree of confidence. There was a minor difficulty with scoring for timing,[45] and a major one with scoring for cer-

---

[44] The certainty scores, which are better indicators of outlook than dating scores, bear out this speculation. The average certainty scores for the two forecasters relying on business cycle indicators were virtually the same for the two peaks together as for the two troughs, whereas for the eight eclectics the average was markedly higher at the two troughs. On accuracy of dating the two using the indicator approach scored markedly higher at the two troughs than at the two peaks, but the disparity was not as great as for the eight eclectics.

[45] For example, one forecast was for a trough in the second quarter of 1958. Since the NBER trough came in April, mechanical application of our methods would have yielded a score of 100, the highest possible. But the actual trough

tainty. All that can be inferred with respect to certainty is whether the score should be above or below 50. If there was a turn in the numerical forecasts of GNP, it could be inferred that the forecaster thought a cyclical turning point was more likely than not, and vice versa, but greater precision was not possible. Another difficulty was that a number of the forecasts in Zarnowitz' sample were made in months for which we did not score our sample.

For two or three of the observations, the average scores for my sample were higher than for Zarnowitz'.[46] In twelve cases, Zarnowitz' scored higher. In the remaining 21 or 22 cases, there was no way to tell which group deserved the higher score.

It appears, therefore, that Zarnowitz' forecasters had greater success in predicting cyclical turns than mine. Such a conclusion, however, rests on a very flimsy foundation. Besides the inadequacies of the data already mentioned, Zarnowitz has found that the mean of a group of forecasts of GNP is superior to most of the individual forecasts entering into the average. Scoring averages for his two groups (in one case the mean, in the other the median) may result in higher scores than would be obtained by averaging scores for each individual forecast in the group.

If we take at face value the conclusion that the forecasters in Zarnowitz' sample were better at recognizing cyclical turns than mine, the superiority may be associated not with a difference of methods but with the facts that (1) my group all published their forecasts, a circumstance that might induce caution about asserting a change in direction, and (2) Zarnowitz' made quantitative, multiperiod forecasts of GNP, a circumstance that kept them from taking refuge in verbal ambiguity.

Of the six forecasts of turns that did not occur in Zarnowitz' sample, one was made in December 1946 for a peak in the second half of that year, one was made in January 1956 for a peak in the first quarter and a trough in the third, and the other four were made in 1962–63. Since the indicators misled some forecasters in both 1956 and 1962–63, there is little ground here for inferring which method is superior with respect to avoiding false signals.

in GNP came not in the second quarter but in the first, so the score given was reduced to 75.

[46] In one case, a different result is obtained depending on whether my sample is deemed to consist of the eight eclectics only or of all ten publications.

9
Conclusions

1. There is a pattern in reports on the business outlook in the vicinity of cyclical peaks and troughs. As time goes by, analysts become increasingly aware of first the possibility, then the probability, and finally the certainty of a turning point. The beginning of this process is almost impossible to date. Forecasters are always aware of the possibility of a turn. Not long before it occurs, their expectation starts to strengthen and to become more definite. The end of the process may come sooner than six months after the turn, as in 1961. On two occasions (the 1949 trough and the 1960 peak) the end of the process cannot be identified. For the majority of forecasters, the process is normally completed in six months.

2. Since World War II, recognition of troughs has been faster than recognition of peaks. Despite the forebodings of an occasional prophet of doom, forecasters have generally expected each contraction to be short and mild. Although they were not able to pinpoint when the trough would come, they were basically right.

3. Geoffrey Moore wrote in 1950, "If the user of statistical indicators could do no better than recognize contemporaneously the turns in general economic activity denoted by our reference dates, he would have a better record than most of his fellows." [47] This study tends to confirm Moore's assertion. Out of seventy-three scores for forecasts made in the month of NBER reference peaks and troughs, there were forty-nine scores of zero for accuracy of dating (67 per cent) and forty scores of less than 50 for degree of certainty (55 per cent).

4. Evidence in this study that users of the NBER indicators approach actually have done better than their fellows is weak. The evidence sug-

[47] *Statistical Indicators of Cyclical Revivals and Recessions,* New York, NBER, 1950, reprinted in *Business Cycle Indicators,* Vol. I, pp. 257–258.

gests, if anything, that relative to other methods the indicators approach may be more sensitive at peaks and less sensitive at troughs. The two analysts covered in this study who relied heavily on the indicators did better than the average of the others in 1957 and 1960 but worse in 1958 and 1961. But, since all analysts use a mixture of methods, this finding is highly tentative. Furthermore, the samples are small and may be unrepresentative.

5. Forecasts have sometimes gone astray as a result of faulty statistical estimates, as in 1947 (industrial production) and 1957 (inventory investment).

6. Business analysts need to (a) state their predictions more precisely and (b) define their subjective estimates of the likelihood of different possibilities. Though the ambiguous language common in reports on business cycles results partly from the nature of the subject, it is associated also with the practice of predicting a single outcome. Under conditions of uncertainty, the single prediction gets hedged, qualified, and fuzzed up. Proper handling of uncertainty requires defining different possibilities and evaluating their likelihood.

Notes to Table A

SOURCES: Garfield V. Cox, *An Appraisal of American Business Forecasts,* rev. ed. (Chicago: The University of Chicago Press, 1930); and Geoffrey H. Moore. For explanation of method, see text, Chapter 3.

[a] One service did not forecast during 1919 trough and 1920 peak; another service began forecasting three months after the 1919 trough; none of the services was available more than four months before the 1919 trough.

[b] Two peaks only for −6, +4, +5, and +6 months; three peaks for −5, −4, −3, −2, and +3 months.

[c] One trough only for +5 and +6 months; two troughs for −6 and +4 months; three troughs for −5, −4, and +3 months.

[d] Detail need not add to total because of rounding.

[e] Scores given represent sixteenths. Possible scores range from −1 to +1 (i.e., from −16 to +16 in terms of numbers shown here).

APPENDIX I

TABLE A

Recognition of Business Cycle Peaks and Troughs, 1919–1929, Six Forecasting Services [a]

	Months Before (−) or After (+) NBER Peak or Trough												
	−6	−5	−4	−3	−2	−1	0	+1	+2	+3	+4	+5	+6
Direction of Change													
4 Peaks [b]													
% Correct	25	24	47	47	53	52	52	57	65	76	55	45	73
% Neutral	58	59	41	47	35	30	30	35	26	18	45	55	18
% Wrong	17	18	12	6	12	17	17	8	8	6	0	0	9
Total [d]	100	100	100	100	100	100	100	100	100	100	100	100	100
4 Troughs [e]													
% Correct	42	44	39	41	41	55	77	77	73	82	64	67	67
% Neutral	58	44	56	55	55	36	18	9	23	18	36	33	33
% Wrong	0	11	6	5	5	9	5	14	5	0	0	0	0
Total [d]	100	100	100	100	100	100	100	100	100	100	100	100	100
8 Peaks and Troughs [b,c]													
% Correct	33	34	43	44	46	53	64	67	69	79	59	53	71
% Neutral	58	51	49	51	46	33	24	22	24	18	41	47	24
% Wrong	8	14	9	5	8	13	11	11	7	3	0	0	6
Total [d]	100	100	100	100	100	100	100	100	100	100	100	100	100
Correctness of Forecasts [e]													
4 Peaks	8	6	2	7	4	5	3	4	7	4	8	7	10
4 Troughs	5	3	4	4	3	7	10	9	12	12	12	11	7
8 Peaks and Troughs	7	5	3	5	3	6	7	7	9	8	10	9	8

TABLE B

Accuracy of Dating Cyclical Peaks and Troughs, 1948–61

Month	Eight Analysts, All Scores		Eight Analysts, Scores Based on Actual Forecasts [a]		"Best" Analyst 1948–61	"Worst" Analyst 1948–61	Two Analysts (Indicators Approach) 1957–61
	Four Troughs	Four Peaks	Four Troughs	Four Peaks			
−3	17	4	23	3	35	0	16
−2	22	6	35	28	31	3	17
−1	29	5	42	17	38	3	20
0	34	6	49	10	47	16	12
1	40	8	54	38	47	35	12
2	43	5	69	36	60	25	25
3	52	5	69	18	60	25	53
4	56	10	81	27	60	25	71
5	68	19	90	53	69	25	76
6	71	23	86	63	72	25	78

[a] Averages shown include positive scores not based on actual forecasts that meet the following conditions: (1) month of forecast +2 or later; (2) forecast of date of turn not revised during scoring period; (3) certainty score in same month 75 or higher. In computing the averages, the individual scores for each month were averaged, and the averages for each month were weighted equally in computing the average shown above.

TABLE C

*Degree of Certainty of Forecasts of Cyclical
Peaks and Troughs, 1948–61*

Month	Eight Analysts		"Best" Analyst 1948–61	"Worst" Analyst 1948–61	Two Analysts (Indicators Approach) 1957–61
	Four Troughs	Four Peaks			
−3	38	21	47	19	30
−2	48	28	58	26	33
−1	52	34	60	25	40
0	53	36	58	29	42
1	61	40	63	40	43
2	69	47	72	45	52
3	81	51	77	54	68
4	87	69	83	67	82
5	94	79	95	68	90
6	97	86	93	73	97

TABLE D

*Comparison of Scores for Accuracy of Dating at Four Peaks
and Four Troughs, 1948–61*
(averages of eight analysts)

Month	Peaks				Troughs			
	1948	1953	1957	1960	1949	1954	1958	1961
−3	0	13	1	0	11	0	29	27
−2	3	13	6	0	19	13	28	29
−1	0	13	6	0	24	25	15	51
0	0	16	6	0	38	29	13	58
1	10	15	6	0	28	35	10	88
2	0	16	4	0	31	40	20	82
3	0	20	0	0	31	48	35	93
4	3	31	5	0	31	53	41	100
5	6	47	22	0	31	63	76	100
6	6	55	22	10	39	65	81	100

TABLE E

*Comparison of Scores for Degree of Certainty at Four Peaks
and Four Troughs, 1948–61*
(averages of eight analysts)

	Peaks				Troughs			
Month	1948	1953	1957	1960	1949	1954	1958	1961
−3	12	25	32	13	29	48	37	37
−2	27	34	32	20	40	61	47	45
−1	34	40	36	25	47	68	41	52
0	37	46	37	23	52	70	40	52
1	45	45	39	28	55	73	45	70
2	52	57	45	32	66	75	57	79
3	53	66	47	38	81	83	71	90
4	72	82	68	52	75	93	83	98
5	80	86	88	60	83	96	95	100
6	90	91	95	70	90	98	98	100

TABLE F

Recognition Scores in Vicinity of 1957 Peak:
Comparison of Indicators Approach with Eclectic Approach

Month	Eight Analysts (Eclectic Approach)	Two Analysts (Indicators Approach)	"Best" Eclectic
Accuracy of Dating			
−3	1	0	0
−2	6	0	0
−1	6	0	0
0	6	0	0
1	6	0	0
2	4	0	0
3	0	0	0
4	5	0	0
5	22	4	75
6	22	13	75
Degree of Certainty			
−3	32	45	35
−2	32	45	10
−1	36	53	15
0	37	50	15
1	39	48	20
2	45	50	35
3	47	63	35
4	68	75	35
5	88	85	95
6	95	98	100

TABLE G

Recognition Scores in Vicinity of 1958 Trough:
Comparison of Indicators Approach with Eclectic Approach

Month	Eight Analysts (Eclectic Approach)	Two Analysts (Indicators Approach)	"Best" Eclectic
	Accuracy of Dating		
−3	29	38	75
−2	28	38	75
−1	15	10	0
0	13	0	75
1	10	0	75
2	20	0	75
3	35	23	75
4	41	100	75
5	76	100	75
6	81	100	100
	Degree of Certainty		
−3	37	28	90
−2	47	30	85
−1	41	30	70
0	40	18	80
1	45	20	85
2	57	35	100
3	71	60	100
4	83	83	100
5	95	93	100
6	98	98	100

TABLE H

Recognition Scores in Vicinity of 1960 Peak:
Comparison of Indicators Approach with Eclectic Approach

Month	Eight Analysts (Eclectic Approach)	Two Analysts (Indicators Approach)	"Best" Eclectic
		Accuracy of Dating	
−3	0	0	0
−2	0	0	0
−1	0	31	0
0	0	0	0
1	0	3	0
2	0	0	0
3	0	90	0
4	0	85	0
5	0	100	0
6	10	100	0
		Degree of Certainty	
−3	13	15	10
−2	20	20	30
−1	25	33	25
0	23	48	20
1	28	48	15
2	32	53	20
3	38	58	35
4	52	75	45
5	60	90	65
6	70	95	40

TABLE I

Recognition Scores in Vicinity of 1961 Trough:
Comparison of Indicators Approach with Eclectic Approach

Month	Eight Analysts (Eclectic Approach)	Two Analysts (Indicators Approach)	"Best" Eclectic
	Accuracy of Dating		
−3	27	25	100
−2	29	31	0
−1	51	38	100
0	58	48	100
1	88	45	100
2	82	100	100
3	93	100	100
4	100	100	100
5	100	100	100
6	100	100	100
	Degree of Certainty		
−3	37	33	75
−2	45	38	85
−1	52	43	85
0	52	50	75
1	70	55	100
2	79	70	100
3	90	90	100
4	98	95	100
5	100	93	100
6	100	98	100

TABLE J

Rankings of Eight Analysts According to Their Mean Certainty
Score at Eight Cyclical Turns [a]

Analysts	Peaks				Troughs			
	1948	1953	1957	1960	1949	1954	1958	1961
A	6	4	5	6	2	3	3	6
Best	4	1	7	7	1	1	1	1
C	7	8	8	8	6	2	8	7
D	3	5	2	2	5	7	6	4
E	1	2	1	1	8	6	4	3
F	2	3	6	3	7	8	2	2
G	8	6	3	4	3	4	4	5
H	5	7	4	5	4	5	7	8

[a] The mean certainty score is an average of the scores over the 10-month span beginning 3 months before the turn and ending 6 months later.

Note: The coefficient of concordance (*W*) measures the degree of consistency among the rankings of the forecasters' performance at each turn. It is defined as

$$W = \frac{S}{\frac{1}{12}m^2(n^3 - n)},$$

where m denotes the number of rankings and n the number of items to be ranked (in the present case, m is the number of turns and n, the number of forecasters), and S denotes the sum of the squares of the deviations about the mean value of the sums of the ranks. S attains a maximum value of $\frac{1}{12}m^2(n^3 - n)$, and $W = 1$, for the case in which the m rankings are identical. That is, if there were perfect consistency, each forecaster would have the same rank for each turn, and W would equal 1. If there were no consistency in the forecasters' performances, W would equal zero. On the theory underlying the measurement of concordance, see M. G. Kendall, *Rank Correlation Methods,* London, 1948, Chapter 6.

For all eight turns, W equals .256; for troughs only, W equals .451; and for peaks only, W equals .622. According to a test based on Fisher's Z-distribution each of these three coefficients is significantly different from zero at the 5 per cent level. This means there is only a 5 per cent probability that the observed consistency in performances arises merely from chance. This test is based on a table given in Milton Friedman, "A Comparison of Alternative Tests of Significance for the Problem of m Rankings," *Annals of Mathematical Statistics,* March 1940 (reprinted in Kendall, *Rank Correlation Methods,* Appendix Table 6).

I am indebted to Rosanne Cole, of the NBER, who performed the test and analyzed the results.

PART II

The Recognition Pattern of the Federal Open Market Committee

by C. ELTON HINSHAW

1
Introduction

This study describes and evaluates the Federal Open Market Committee's performance in anticipating and recognizing seven post-World War II cyclical turns, and relates the FOMC's policy actions to its views of economic conditions in the vicinity of these turns. One aspect of the controversy concerning the efficacy of countercyclical monetary policy has been the Federal Reserve's promptness or lag in recognizing the need for action when a peak or trough in general business occurs. Two previous studies assessing the Federal Reserve System's ability to recognize business cycle turning points reached conflicting conclusions. For the cyclical turns since the 1951 Accord, Kareken and Solow estimated the recognition lag—the period between the turn and the Federal Reserve's recognition of it—to be approximately 8.5 months at peaks and three months at troughs.[1] Brunner and Meltzer disagreed. They concluded that:

"In current academic parlance, the 'inside lag' of monetary policy appears to be extremely short. On two of the three occasions when the economy turned toward recession, the 'recognition lag' was negative; when the economy turned toward recovery, the 'recognition lag' was longer, averaging 3 to 4 months." [2]

---

[1] John Kareken and Robert M. Solow, "Lags in Monetary Policy," in *Stabilization Policies,* Englewood Cliffs, N. J., 1963, p. 70. The total lag of monetary policy can conveniently be divided into an inside, an intermediate, and an outside lag. The inside lag is usually defined as the period between the need for action and the taking of action, and can conceptually be partitioned into a recognition lag (the period between the need for action and its recognition) and the decision or action lag (the period between recognition and the taking of action). Since the Federal Reserve has the power to act when the need is recognized, Kareken and Solow assumed that the decision lag was zero or negligible and that the inside lag was essentially a recognition lag.

The intermediate lag is defined as the period between the taking of action and the financial effects of the action, and the outside lag as the period between the financial impact and its effect on real production and employment. See *ibid.,* pp. 3 and 62.

[2] Karl Brunner and A. H. Meltzer, *The Federal Reserve's Attachment to the*

Both studies determined the Federal Reserve's recognition lag by comparing the National Bureau of Economic Research (NBER) dates of business cycle turns with dates of "policy change." [3] The maximum amount of earning assets that member banks as a group could hold was used by Kareken and Solow as their indicator of modification in monetary policy; the lag in the change in trend of this policy index behind the NBER business cycle dates was their measure of the recognition lag. Brunner and Meltzer inferred recognition by comparing the NBER dates with a score assigned to the Federal Reserve's actions. Using a scale ranging from $+1$ (decisive easing) to -1 (decisive tightening), they each independently scored the FOMC's actions as given in the "Record of Policy Actions," a section in the Federal Reserve Board's *Annual Reports*. They then compared scores and arrived at a consensus score which presumably reflected the Committee's view of current and expected economic conditions. After comparing their scores of the Committee's actions with the dates of cyclical turns, they concluded that "the System's post-Accord record of recognizing and acting at turning points can only be regarded as splendid." [4]

Since these studies were completed, the Federal Open Market Committee's minutes for 1936–60 [5] have become available, and it is now possible to ascertain directly what the Committee thought about current and future economic conditions for seven of the postwar turns. Attempting to assess the Committee's ability to recognize cyclical turns by inference from policy changes alone can be misleading. Only if the FOMC reversed the direction of policy solely upon anticipation or recognition of peaks or troughs would this approach yield satisfactory results. If the Committee changes policy for other reasons, as it did in

Free Reserve Concept, Subcommittee on Domestic Finance, House of Representatives, 88th Congress, 2d Sess., Washington, 1964, p. 50.

[3] The NBER chronology of business cycle dates provides a record of cyclical turns that shows the month in which the peak or trough is judged to have occurred. See Table II-1 for the NBER reference cycle dates for the peaks and troughs covered in this study.

[4] *Ibid.*, p. 50. The "Accord" referred to is the Treasury-Federal Reserve Accord of 1951.

[5] Federal Open Market Committee, *Minutes of the Committee, 1936–60, and Its Executive Committee, 1936–55,* The National Archives, Washington, 1964. (Hereafter referred to as *Minutes.*) Prior to 1947, meetings of the Committee were so infrequent and discussions of economic conditions so sparse that an adequate comparison between the 1937–38 turns and the postwar turns could not be made. Consequently the study is limited to the 1947–60 period.

the 1947–60 period,[6] the question arises as to whether such action is in response to an expected (or recognized) turning point or for some other purpose (i.e., "disorderly markets," balance of payments problems, etc.). The Committee's minutes are the best source of this information. A reading of these minutes shows that a modification of the previous findings is in order. The minutes yield additional information about the Committee's ability to recognize cyclical turns and, in combination with its actions, yield additional insight into decisions concerning monetary policy.

Chapter 2 describes the method used to evaluate the Committee's forecasts. Chapter 3 reviews chronologically the FOMC's view of economic conditions in the vicinity of the seven postwar turns covered by its minutes and compares its ability to recognize peaks and troughs with that of the business analysts studied by Fels. Chapter 4 relates the Committee's forecasts and views of current economic conditions to the policy decisions which it made during the periods surrounding cyclical turns. And the impatient reader can turn to Chapter 5 for the conclusions.

2

Procedure

In his study of the problem of forecasting and recognizing business cycle peaks and troughs, Fels found "there is a pattern in reports on the business outlook in the vicinity of cyclical peaks and troughs. As time goes by, analysts become increasingly aware of first the possibility, then the probability, and finally the certainty of a turning point." [7]

[6] Brunner and Meltzer recorded eighty-seven changes in policy during the years 1947–60. See their *An Alternative Approach to the Monetary Mechanism,* Subcommittee on Domestic Finance, House of Representatives, 88th Congress, 2d Sess., Washington, 1964, pp. 119–124.

[7] Rendigs Fels, "The Recognition Patterns of Business Analysts," the companion piece in this volume. Fels studied the forecasts of ten publications made in the vicinity of the eight turning points since World War II. Only eight of the publi-

That is, recognition of a cyclical turn does not suddenly occur after a discrete lag. Rather, there is a pattern of recognition beginning with the first vague indications of awareness of the possibility of a turn. As new information becomes available, more or less confidence is shown that a peak or trough is approaching (or has passed) and eventually, if the turn occurs, the forecaster becomes certain.

How does the FOMC's views of economic conditions in the vicinity of cyclical turns compare with those of other forecasters? Does policy responsibility influence the Committee's outlook? To answer these questions systematically, statements indicative of the members' views have been excerpted from the Committee's minutes for the period 1947–60. Beginning three months before the NBER reference cycle date and ending six months afterwards, these quotations were scored using the system developed by Fels.[8]

1. The Scoring System

The scores can range from zero to 100 per cent in 5 per cent increments, and are assigned on the following basis. The Committee members always have some opinion about the likelihood of a peak or trough that can be expressed in the form of a percentage, though the percentages are usually implicit. Each score assigned represents the scorers' estimate of the likelihood implicit in the Committee's discussions of a cyclical turn within a three-month target interval centered on the NBER business cycle date. The three-month target interval is used as a time dimension restriction on the forecast. The longer the time period to which a forecast refers, the more confident a forecaster would be that a peak or trough would occur. If the time period were sufficiently long, one would expect a cyclical turn with 100 per cent confidence. Each assigned score represents the scorers' answer to the question: "What is the probability of a

cations were available for the entire period. The use of his findings in this study is restricted to those eight (four business publications, two security services, and two bank letters), and to seven of the eight turns. The February 1961 turn is omitted here because at the time the study was completed the FOMC *Minutes* had been published only through 1960.

[8] Although Fels used two kinds of scores, one for timing and one for degree of certainty, only the scoring procedure for certainty is used in this study. The Committee's comments on timing of cyclical turns were so few that an adequate comparison between the scores at various turns and between the Committee and the business forecasters could not be made.

cyclical turn within plus or minus one month of the NBER business cycle date implicit in this forecast?" A score of zero is assigned to a forecast implying virtual certainty (less than 2.5 per cent chance) that no turn will (did) occur within the target interval.

Following the procedure used by Fels, the "normal chance" of a peak within any three-month period is assumed to be 10 per cent; of a trough, 15 per cent. These percentages are rough approximations based on the historical averages of peacetime expansions (two to three years) and contractions (about one and one-half years). Since forecasters are virtually always aware of some possibility of a turn, the "normal chance" score is assigned (10 per cent in the vicinity of peaks, 15 per cent in the vicinity of troughs) unless the Committee's discussion implies that the chances are greater or less than "normal." If the Committee's discussion of economic conditions indicates a greater than "normal chance" of a cyclical turn within the three-month interval centered on the NBER business cycle date, a higher score is assigned—up to the maximum of 100 per cent. A score of 100 per cent implies virtual certainty (likelihood greater than 97.5 per cent) that a turn did (will) occur within the target interval. Since the scores are subjective evaluations of the Committee's discussions, they are limited to multiples of five (i.e., there are twenty-one possible scores). No finer gradation is justified.

To indicate better the nature of the scoring procedure, a few quotations from the minutes and the score which would be assigned to each are in order.

The following statements would be given the "normal chance" score for peaks and troughs, respectively:

Almost all recent data continue to reflect rapid economic growth. Even with a steel strike of relatively long duration, the present momentum of economic recovery will almost certainly continue to carry the economy higher . . .[9] (Score—10 per cent.)

Recent statistical data confirm the continued business decline, and there is no sign yet of any combination of favorable factors sufficiently strong to reverse this trend.[10] (Score—15 per cent.)

A score of 50 per cent, which implies that the forecaster believes that a turn within the target interval is as likely as not, would be assigned to the following statements:

[9] *Minutes,* July 28, 1959, p. 509.
[10] *Ibid.,* March 4, 1958, p. 176.

Whether this is a period of formation of forces for further uptrend or for some downward readjustment can not yet be clearly read from current business indicators.[11]

I believe that a generally sidewise movement of the economy is more likely during the next few months than a pronounced and cumulative movement either up or down.[12]

The economy is in a more or less neutral and uncertain area between expansion and recession.[13]

A score of 100 per cent implies that the forecaster was certain that a peak or trough had occurred. The following comments by members of the FOMC would receive that score:

Data becoming available made it clear that a vigorous economic recovery was now visible and tangible.[14] (Score with respect to preceding trough—100 per cent.)

In recent reports to the Committee, I have used the words "downsettling" to characterize the drift in over-all activity. In the light of recent information, general economic recession now appears to be the most appropriate description.[15] (Score with respect to preceding peak—100 per cent.)

The unfolding data are abundantly clear. They show vigorous revival— one of the more robust on record following one of history's shorter and milder contraction periods.[16] (Score with respect to preceding trough— 100 per cent.)

Although as many as twenty different views may be expressed at any one meeting, only one score is assigned. The Committee is considered to be a single forecaster. To determine how well a single score for the entire Committee reflected the opinions of the members, the author scored each individual's forecast separately in the vicinity of the 1960 peak. The individual scores for each meeting were then averaged; this mean score represents the degree of certainty for the Committee as a whole for that meeting. After a lapse of time sufficient to forget the previously determined scores the author assigned one score per meeting to the entire Committee as a single forecaster. For each meeting, the average score for all forecasts and the single score for the Committee as a whole were compared.

The two patterns of certainty scores were quite similar until five and

[11] *Ibid.*, August 25, 1953, p. 318.
[12] *Ibid.*, September 22, 1954, pp. 277–78.
[13] *Ibid.*, September 13, 1960, pp. 706–708.
[14] *Ibid.*, December 28, 1954, p. 395.
[15] *Ibid.*, December 12, 1957, p. 770.
[16] *Ibid.*, August 19, 1958, p. 692.

six months after the turn (see Appendix II, Table C), at which time the score for the Committee as a whole became substantially larger than the mean score of the individual forecasts. This divergence in the patterns may be attributed to the author's intuitive weighting of the forecasts of those members who analyzed the outlook in detail and stated precisely what they viewed the situation to be. In making policy decisions, those whose views are not yet crystalized may be strongly influenced by members who are positive. A single score for the whole Committee permits intuitive weighting of the views expressed and gives a clear, though subjective, picture of the Committee's outlook. In addition, it is not clear that an unweighted average of individual scores would be appropriate. Since everyone (seven Governors, twelve Presidents, and several staff members) attending the meeting may express an opinion but only the twelve members can vote, should all forecasts be treated equally? If not, how should the relative weights be assigned? Any weighted average score would involve as much subjectivity as a single score for the Committee as a whole.[17] Consequently, for the remaining months only one score for each meeting was assigned.

When there were two or more meetings in a month, the scores for each meeting were consolidated into a single score for the month. When there was no meeting in a given month, the score was derived by interpolation. This procedure facilitated comparisons of the FOMC's recognition patterns for different turns and comparisons of its patterns with those of the eight business analysts studied by Fels.

As a check on the author's interpretation of the Committee's forecasts, John Pilgrim, a graduate student, independently scored the excerpted quotes using the same procedure. We then compared scores. If a simple average of the two scores did not seem representative of either person's interpretation of the minutes, we discussed the forecasts and reached a consensus score, which is the score used in this study.[18]

[17] Pragmatically, the time required to score each person's comments individually for all seven turns would have been prohibitive, but it was done for the 1960 peak to gauge how much difference the procedure used makes in the recognition pattern.

[18] The original sets of independent scores are available upon request. In general, the patterns revealed by the independent scores were similar, and no important conclusion would be altered by the use of either of the original sets of scores rather than the consensus score. More than a third of the independent scores were identical, and nearly all the rest differed by 5 points or less. Pilgrim's scores were higher than the author's more often than not.

Although the scoring method glosses over differences in opinion among the individual members of the Committee and changes in the Committee's view in meetings within the same month, we believe the resulting certainty scores are sufficiently indicative of the Committee's views on past, current, and future economic conditions to justify the conclusions based on them.

From this pattern of certainty scores two values have been selected as being of particular use in assessing the Committee's ability to discern cyclical turns—the 50 per cent score and the 90 per cent score. The period between a turn and the first score of more than 50 per cent for the Committee's forecasts is defined as the recognition lag. Notice that this definition of "recognition" is independent of any policy decision which the Committee may have made and, therefore, is not comparable to "recognition" as defined in either of the previous studies. A score of 50 implies that the FOMC believes that a turn within the target interval (the NBER business cycle date plus or minus one month) is as likely as not. It does not imply or depend upon any "policy action," but is based on the Committee's new view of economic conditions.

The period between a turn and a score of 90 per cent, which implies a great degree of certainty that a turn has occurred, is defined as the confirmation lag.[19]

2. Standard of Comparison

An appropriate way to evaluate the ability of the FOMC to recognize and confirm cyclical turns is to compare its performance with that of other forecasters. The forecasting performances of the eight business analysts studied by Fels serve as a basis for this evaluation.

Beginning three months before the NBER business cycle date of a

[19] Appendix II, Table C, which compares unweighted average scores of individual's comments with the single scores for the Committee, raises a question concerning this criterion. Since at five and six months after the peak the single scores for the FOMC are substantially higher than the unweighted average scores, is the 90 per cent criterion large enough to warrant the conclusion that the Committee "confirmed" the occurrence of a turn? A 95 per cent criterion would affect the "confirmation" lag at only one turn—the 1960 peak. But a 100 per cent standard would extend the confirmation lag at all peaks, except 1957, beyond the six-month period; the lag at the troughs of 1954 and 1958 would be increased by one month each, and the lag at the 1949 trough would be increased by two months (see Appendix II, Table A). Given the subjective nature of the scoring procedure, the author felt that a certainty score of 90 per cent indicated a sufficiently high degree of confidence to justify its use as the criterion for "confirmation."

turn and ending six months after the turn, the Committee's certainty scores are compared with those of the eight business publications. These ten scores reflect the varying estimates of the forecasters' ability to recognize the occurrence of the turn as it is approached and passed. Two comparisons are made: the first compares the Committee's certainty scores with the average scores of the eight business forecasters; the second compares the Committee's recognition pattern with that of the "best" forecaster of the eight. The "best" forecaster is the publication with the highest mean certainty score for all postwar turns and is the same publication selected by Fels as his "best" forecaster. Its performance in recognizing troughs primarily accounts for its high over-all certainty score. The publication had the highest mean certainty score at each of the four troughs, but its performance was only the fourth best of the eight forecasters in recognizing peaks. Moreover, its position at peaks would be lower but for its exceptional performance at one peak, 1953. Hence in terms of consistency of performance the "best" forecaster is by no means the best, and indeed it strongly suggests an optimistic bias.

To check the consistency of the forecasters' performances, each of the eight publications in Fels' sample was ranked according to its performance at each of the eight turns. For all eight turns, for troughs only and for peaks only, the coefficient of concordance (which measures the degree of consistency among the rankings) is significantly different from zero at the five per cent confidence level.[20] Hence there is some evidence of consistency in the forecasters' performance, but the results for peaks and troughs separately may imply merely that some forecasters have an optimistic and others a pessimistic bias, while the results for peaks and troughs together may be attributed as much to forecasts that are consistently poor as to forecasts that are consistently good. Since the forecaster with the best over-all average record also has a highly variable and apparently biased performance, comparisons of the Committee's record with that of the "best" forecaster must be heavily qualified.

3. False Alarms

In order to check for false alarms—the "recognition" of turns which did not occur—and to obtain an estimate of the significance of scores

[20] See Appendix I, Table J for more detail.

the number of months before the NBER date of the turn by which the Committee was judged to have begun recognizing an approaching turn. In three cases the pattern began more than three months before the turn, but for only two (1953 and 1957) did it begin substantially before that time. In each of these cases, the year previous to the peak year had been a period in which the Committee exhibited considerable concern about the possibility of a turn (see the above discussion of "false alarms"). As a rule of thumb, three months prior to a turn seems to be a reasonable date for the beginning of recognition, and comparisons of the FOMC's recognition pattern with that of the business forecasters is made on this basis.

3

The FOMC's Recognition Pattern: A Chronological Review

To give the reader more insight into the forecasting ability of the Committee than is provided by the certainty scores alone, this section describes its recognition pattern for each of the seven postwar turns covered in this study and compares its performance in recognizing and confirming these with the performances of the forecasters in Fels' sample of eight.

When policy actions are referred to, the author adopted the language of the Committee in characterizing them. For example, the "policy of neutrality" is the Committee's terminology, not the author's. Consequently, the references to "easy," "tight," "neutral," etc., money policies do not necessarily represent the author's opinion as to what monetary policy was being pursued, but represent the Committee's intentions as indicated in its minutes. Such references are merely descriptive and, as noted above, the scoring of the FOMC's forecasts is independent of the actions taken.

1. The 1948 Peak

With the expiration of wartime price controls in the second half of 1946, an inflation began that dominated the economy from 1946 to late 1948. Throughout 1947 and 1948 monetary policy was designed to keep pressure on member bank reserves and to restrain the further expansion of bank credit. However, because of the wartime growth of the public debt and because of its responsibility for maintaining an orderly market for government securities at low interest rates, the Federal Reserve was unable to restrain credit expansion to the desired extent and acted as a "permissive parent" of the inflation.

Inflationary pressures paused twice over the three-year period of expansion: once in the second quarter of 1947 when businesses began disinvesting in inventories, and again in early 1948 when commodity prices broke sharply downward. The Committee indicated little concern that the first lull in the pace of inflation might be the beginning or forewarning of recession. It viewed the pause as temporary relief from persistent inflationary pressures.[22] In contrast, Fels found that the lull "was widely misinterpreted as the beginning of recession" by many analysts.[23] During the second pause, the Committee took a "wait and see" attitude as to whether the decline in commodity prices was the signal of a major adjustment or simply a needed correction of a particular situation. The consensus was that, despite the price break, the basic inflationary forces were still at work.[24] Again some business commentators "raised the question of recession prematurely." [25]

The downturn began in the fourth quarter of 1948. The NBER's business cycle peak is November. At its October meeting, the Committee appraised the situation as inflationary and recommended a continuing anti-inflationary program.[26] Their comments show that the Committee members had little premonition that a cyclical peak was imminent. During November the FOMC recognized a hesitation in business ac-

[22] *Minutes,* June 5, 1947, pp. 102ff.
[23] Part I of this volume, p. 26.
[24] *Minutes,* February 26 and 27, 1948, pp. 24–49.
[25] Part I, p. 26.
[26] *Minutes,* October 4, 1948, pp. 165–72. John H. Williams, a staff member, expressed the very perceptive opinion, as summarized in the minutes, that "inflation was in the process of wearing itself out, that the prospect was for moving sidewise or even downward, that a serious downturn was unlikely." (*Ibid.,* p. 166.)

tivity but viewed the weakness as temporary and felt that the basic expansionary forces continued unchanged.[27] Over the next three months, there was a gradual drift toward pessimism about the future direction of the economy. By March 1949, the Committee regarded the economic situation as a "healthy readjustment" which would be helpful in bringing greater stability to the economy. Its feeling was that a moderate adjustment could prevent a precipitous downward spiral in the future. It wished to encourage what was viewed as a helpful development, and changed from a policy of restraint to one of "neutrality." [28] The Committee felt "it should replace the existing policy of exercising restraint on credit expansion with a policy which would relax such restraint without following an aggressive easy money policy." [29]

During April and May the FOMC continued to adjust policy in the direction of ease as it became increasingly confident that the "healthy readjustment" was turning into cyclical recession. But it was not until June that the Committee confirmed that the economy was actually in the midst of a recession. They agreed that "declines in business in recent months had gone faster than had been considered likely at the beginning of the year, [and] that further declines appeared probable. . . . Now the time has come for an affirmative credit policy in the light of the developing business situation, which would have significance to the market, the banking system, and ourselves." [30]

Relative to the NBER business cycle peak date of November, 1948, this means that the lag in confirming the occurrence of the downturn was some seven months—the Committee's poorest performance during the period studied. The recognition patterns of the FOMC and other business analysts were quite similar (Chart II-1). For the Committee, the scores for this peak were the lowest for any of the seven turns; for the business analysts, scores for recognition were lower than for any other turn except 1960. The business forecasters did not "recognize" (i.e., did not receive a score greater than 50) until two months after the NBER date of the peak; the Committee received such a score only three months afterwards. Neither group had "confirmed" (i.e., received a score of 90 or better) by the end of six months. For the Committee this was the only turn that was not confirmed within a six-month period.

[27] *Minutes,* November 15, 1948, pp. 180–183.
[28] *Ibid.,* March 1, 1949, pp. 44–50.
[29] *Annual Report of the Board of Governors of the Federal Reserve System, 1949,* p. 111.
[30] *Minutes,* June 28, 1949, pp. 82–83.

CHART II-1

Certainty Scores for the November 1948 Peak

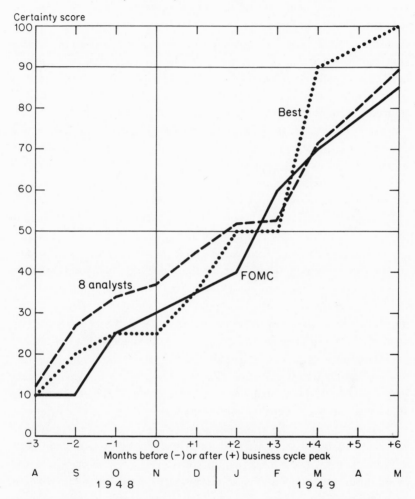

Certainty score

SOURCE: Part I of this study and other original data made available to the author.

Although the recognition performance of the "best" forecasting publication was inferior to that of the average of the eight in the immediate vicinity of the peak, it is interesting to note that it confirmed the occurrence of the turn in March—the month of policy change by the Committee. Was it, perhaps, strongly influenced by the FOMC's decision to ease?

What accounts for the relatively poor performances in recognizing the cyclical changes taking place in 1948? Fels hypothesized that forecasters (1) did not realize the extent to which the structure of the economic system had changed as a result of the depression and the war, (2) became cautious after misinterpreting the lull in 1947 as the beginning of recession and repeated the error in early 1948, (3) wondered if the decline might be followed by another bout of inflation, and (4) thought in terms of deep depression and rapid inflation rather than business cycles with mild contractions.[31]

Most of these factors influenced the Committee. The recession that occurred was not the expected depression. Although the widely held expectation of a severe contraction following the war proved groundless, the FOMC felt that continued inflation would only make the ultimate adjustments more severe. Twice before, the economy had halted its inflationary expansion, and these postponements of the contraction could only make the inevitable downswing deeper. The decline that did occur was so mild relative to expectations that it was considered a "healthy readjustment" which would reduce the inevitable reaction following three years of almost continuous inflation. The Committee was aware that government expenditures were to increase sharply. This, in combination with the tax cut in the spring of 1948 and the newly adopted role of the government in attempting to stabilize economic activity, led to expectations of continued expansion over the near term.

In addition, however, the FOMC was particularly concerned about inflation because of its inability to restrict credit to the desired extent. Its responsibility for pegging interest rates on government securities left the Committee with little room to maneuver against inflationary pressures and made its members acutely aware of their inability to restrain credit expansion. They were increasingly conscious of inflationary developments after experiencing almost three years of frustration in trying to slow down the expansion of credit. The Committee's concern with the problem of halting inflation led it to neglect the developing recession.

2. The 1949 Trough

The eleven-month contraction was very mild. In constant (1958) dollars, GNP declined from a peak of $328.7 billion in the fourth quarter

[31] See Part I of this volume.

of 1948 to a low of $323.3 billion in the fourth quarter of 1949. The trough was double-bottomed. A recovery began in July only to be interrupted by the coal and steel strikes in September and early October, but the lull was short and expansion resumed when the strikes ended. The second trough in October is the one selected by the NBER as the business cycle date.

At its August meeting, the Committee agreed that "as long as the condition of declining economic activity continued the System should see to it that conditions of monetary ease and low money rates were maintained as a means of encouraging business activity." [32] In September the Committee "recognized" the cyclical turn and a score of 60 was assigned to the forecasts. It felt that the expansion of business activity during July and August probably indicated that the end of recession was near but decided that nascent recovery was too precarious to warrant a change in the direction of policy. Indicative comments were:

> If the signs of developing business recovery which were apparent during July and August had begun to accelerate and give indication of an end of the present period of adjustment, there might be some reason for reexamining the policies adopted by the System in June, but . . . it had become clear that the recovery was rather precarious and . . . an adjustment still had to take place in the price structure.[33]

> In view of the recent and continuing recovery in business activity, the present did not seem . . . to be an appropriate time to make the reduction in discount rates.[34]

The Executive Committee of the FOMC "confirmed" the revival in business conditions at their November meeting and advocated a shift in policy toward restraint. Allan Sproul stated that "it appeared to be the consensus of the System economists that present business conditions would continue at about existing high levels through the first half of 1950, . . . and the high levels of business activity were re-introducing an inflationary bias in the economy. . . ." [35] Marriner Eccles' opinion was that "the System should give some indication through a firming of short-term rates that it had recognized the change in conditions that had taken place in recent months." [36] The Committee agreed that continued

[32] *Minutes,* August 5, 1949, pp. 112–113.
[33] *Ibid.,* September 21, 1949, p. 145.
[34] *Ibid.,* p. 148.
[35] *Ibid.,* November 18, 1949, p. 156.
[36] *Ibid.,* pp. 156–157.

expansion was expected and that a more restrictive credit policy should be followed.

Of all turns, the average certainty score for the 1949 trough is the highest. If the NBER business cycle date is used as the criterion, the Committee "confirmed" the reversal only one month after it occurred and "recognized" the turn one month before it occurred. However, it is clear that the Committee felt that the cyclical turn occurred in July. The coal and steel strike which interrupted the revival in October was not viewed as a sufficient force to break the economy's continued upward movement. If the alternative date of the trough (July) is used, then the confirmation lag is four months and the recognition lag two months. In either case, the FOMC was much more prompt in correctly assessing the situation than were the business analysts (see Chart II-2). Fels found that "among troughs, the scores for 1949 are lowest, though the difference from 1958 is slight. The scores might have been even lower for 1949 had the trough not been double-bottomed." [37] Indeed, it was not until April 1950, that the business analysts reached an average score of 90 per cent (i.e., "confirmed" the occurrence of the trough), some five months after the FOMC. Although the "best" forecasting publication did significantly better than the average of the eight, it did not match the FOMC in confirming the turn. In light of the performance of others for recognizing and confirming the 1949 trough, the Committee's performance was remarkable. The discounting of the deflationary impact of the strikes undoubtedly accounts for most of the superiority of the FOMC over the other forecasters.

3. The 1953 Peak

Following the 1949 trough, the economy began an expansion, dominated by developments associated with the Korean war, which carried GNP to a record level of $367.5 billion in the second quarter of 1953. During all of 1950 and through the first half of 1951 the Federal Reserve continued and intensified its policy of credit restraint. However, as 1951 progressed, the inflationary pressures slackened and the outlook became one of approximate balance at a high level of activity. Beginning in June, the Committee changed to a policy of "neutrality."

As the economy continued expanding through 1952 and into 1953,

[37] See Part I, pp. 26–27.

CHART II-2

Certainty Scores for the October 1949 Trough

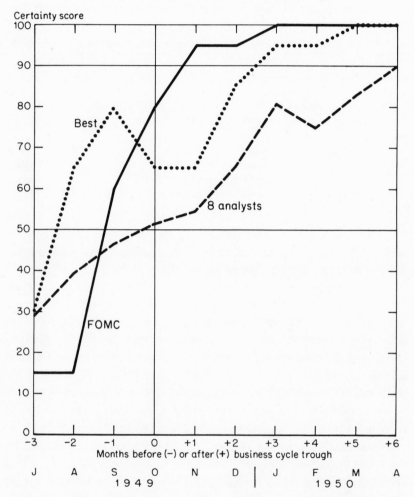

Certainty score

Months before (−) or after (+) business cycle trough

J   A   S   O   N   D | J   F   M   A
1 9 4 9   1 9 5 0

SOURCE: Part I of this study and other original data made available to the author.

and its need for money and credit grew with increasing activity, the policy of neutrality gradually became a policy of restraint. A gradual shift in the viewpoint of the Committee occurred during the first quarter of 1953: there was a growing concern that the expansion might develop into an unsustainable boom which would eventually result in downward adjustments. The Committee unanimously agreed that open market operations should be conducted so as not to encourage ease.[38]

Pessimism about the future course of business activity increased during April and May; there was a change of emphasis in open market operations, from a policy designed "not to encourage ease" to one intending "to keep the market tight but to keep it from getting any tighter." [39] The comment which typified the Committee's view was that:

> The Open Market Committee's policy of credit neutrality gradually became a policy of credit restraint and, with a further lag, has become a tight money policy . . .
> The necessitous borrowing of the Treasury will press further on bank reserves, and put further pressure on the money market if we do nothing to offset it. It would be appropriate to buy government securities to prevent this Treasury borrowing from introducing new pressures upon bank reserves.[40]

The Committee decided that, in light of the existing tightness and the needs of the Treasury, some reserves should be injected into the market in order to keep it from becoming too tight.[41]

At its June meeting, the FOMC agreed that there should be a further increase in reserves in the near future. The Committee injected reserves into the market primarily because of the existing tightness and the anticipated disorderly market in government securities, and only secondarily because of some concern about the near-term condition of business activity.

At the June meeting the Committee's staff review stated that economic conditions were "characterized by a moderately higher level of economic activity and generally stable prices. While the economic situation has continued strong, financial markets have been unsettled at times and throughout the period there has been an undertone of concern about potential declines in economic activity." [42] After an extended discussion of "disorderly markets," the Committee members agreed that reserves should be injected into the market on a sharply rising basis in order to keep the situation from getting tighter.[43] Although their discus-

[38] *Minutes,* March 24, 1953, p. 106.
[39] *Ibid.,* May 26, 1953, p. 191.
[40] *Ibid.,* May 6, 1953, p. 147.
[41] *Ibid.,* pp. 147–158.
[42] *Ibid.,* June 11, 1953, pp. 199–200.
[43] *Ibid.,* pp. 240–244.

sion indicates that they were aware of the changing business conditions, they did not view the situation as the beginning of cyclical contraction. We assigned a certainty score of 45.

During July and August, after the Treasury financing program was out of the way, the FOMC decided that only token purchases should be made for the System's account. This is further evidence that the possibility of a peak was only a marginal factor in the decision to inject reserves during June. The staff review in August typifies the viewpoint of the Committee concerning the future outlook:

> Record levels of aggregate output and employment attained in the second quarter of 1953 have generally been maintained thus far in the current quarter; . . . the situation continued to be characterized by over-all stability in prices and activity and by considerable selectivity in developments in particular lines; and . . . whether this is a period of formation of forces for further uptrend or for some downward readjustment can not yet be clearly read from current business indicators.[44]

The Committee members viewed the near-term outlook as one of continued horizontal movement at high levels and they were trying to keep the balance between inflationary and deflationary developments. In light of their discussion, we assigned a score of 50 to the August meeting.

At the September meeting, a policy of active ease was begun. The Committee was not yet convinced that recession was underway but considered the probability of renewed inflation to be small. From a balance between inflationary and deflationary forces, the Committee's outlook changed to a balance between stability and deflationary forces. Although the initiation of such a policy makes it apparent that the Committee recognized the probability of deflationary forces gaining the upper hand (the certainty score was 70), it was not until January 1954 that the July peak was actually confirmed as the beginning of a recession in business activity.

Among the four peaks, the FOMC's performance in recognizing the 1953 turn was the best. The same is true for the business analysts and for the "best" forecaster of the eight.[45] Although the recognition patterns of the average of the forecasters and the Committee were quite similar, the "best" forecaster did significantly better (see Chart II-3). Several months before the peak both groups evidenced concern about the level

[44] *Ibid.,* August 25, 1953, p. 318.
[45] Part I, p. 28, and other original data made available to the author.

CHART II-3

Certainty Scores for the July 1953 Peak

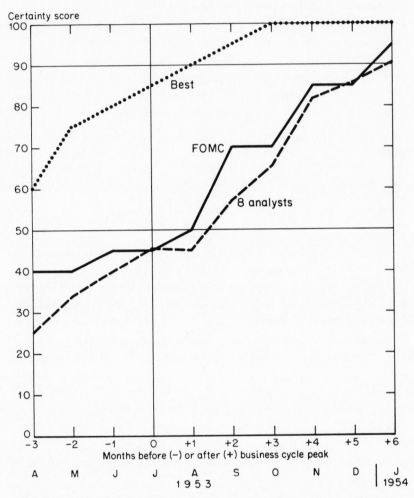

SOURCE: Part I of this study and other original data made available to the author.

of activity during the second half of 1953.[46] In anticipating changing business conditions, the Committee did well. However, as the peak approached and passed, definite realization that recession was, in fact, occurring increased only slowly, as Chart II-3 indicates. Several reasons could account for such a pattern of recognition.

The downswing was relatively easy to anticipate. The end of the Korean war was not difficult to foresee and the reduction in defense expenditures was anticipated. Such expenditures had been a mainstay through most of the expansion. This time there were no accumulated private demands as a result of war shortages and no accumulated liquid assets to fill the gap. Indeed, in several areas (i.e., consumer durables, plant and equipment, and housing) private demands had been stable or declining since early 1951. Consequently no good reason existed to expect continued expansion once defense expenditures were cut.

In addition, the FOMC had already taken action to ease pressure in the money market before the peak occurred. In June, a month before the NBER business cycle peak, the Committee injected substantial amounts of reserves into the market to avoid further tightening. The members realized that their policy of neutrality had gradually become a policy of restraint and then of undue tightness as the economy continued to expand. The fear of failure of the Treasury debt issue and the uncertainty of the business outlook led them to ease credit conditions. Consequently, since action had already been taken, the Committee was under no real pressure to confirm the "slippage" in economic activity as nascent recession and to reverse the direction of policy. In addition, the recession was so mild that euphemisms such as "horizontal movement at a high level," and "slippage" were not unfounded.

Whatever the reasons for the slow confirmation, the Committee must be given credit for a good early warning of the peak. The FOMC took appropriate action, however gratuitous, prior to the turn in business activity and probably modified the severity of the subsequent recession.

---

[46] Two members of the Committee made excellent forecasts as early as the fall of 1952. In October, C. R. Youngdahl, a staff member, described the outlook as "one in which we are looking toward a period of downward adjustment next spring or after mid-1953, while rather strong business activity is indicated for the period immediately ahead." (*Minutes,* October 22, 1952, p. 194.) And in November, C. S. Young said: "While a good level of business activity was anticipated through the first quarter of 1953 . . . there was considerable sentiment that some decline would occur after that, partly because it was anticipated that defense expenditures would decline." (*Ibid.,* November 5, 1952, p. 202.)

4. The 1954 Trough

The contraction lasted thirteen months—from July 1953 until August
1954. During the first half of 1954, consumer expenditures became an
expansionary force. One of the primary factors supporting the rise in
consumption was the increase in disposable income as a result of the
January 1954 tax cut. The revival of consumer expenditures, the continued expansion of state and local government spending, and the
stability of fixed investment soon brought the contraction to a halt and
the economy moved sidewise through most of the second and third
quarters of 1954. The recovery began in September.

As the recession continued into 1954 with little evidence of either an
upswing or a leveling off, the Committee continued its policy of active
ease through the first quarter of 1954. In April there was a slight drift
toward optimism as the recession seemed to be slowing down, and by
May the consensus was that the economy was beginning to level off.
Indicative comments were:

> Unless the downward drift was reinforced by fresh contractive factors,
> activity might be approaching a balanced position at current moderately re-
> duced levels. While the foundations of revival might be taking shape, the
> sources of revival impetus were not yet clear.[47]
> The decline had begun to level off but whether it is a U or V bottom,
> or just a ledge in a downward drift, we can not yet know.[48]
> The current decline in economic activity had about leveled off. . . .[49]

In June it was apparent that the rate of decline in activity had slowed
and the "leveling off" thesis was maintained by the Committee with little
increase in confidence as to the future outlook. The active ease policy
was continued through the entire second quarter.

The outlook had improved somewhat by the beginning of the third
quarter and the Committee was assigned a score of 50 (see Chart II-4).
The drift toward optimism began in July. The typical view was expressed by staff member Frank R. Garfield when he said, as summarized in the minutes, "during June economic developments continued
to show mixed trends with further indications that recessionary tendencies were abating but no clear evidence that an upturn was under

[47] *Minutes,* May 11, 1954, pp. 147–148.
[48] *Ibid.,* p. 150.
[49] *Ibid.,* May 26, 1954, p. 159.

CHART II-4

Certainty Scores for the August 1954 Trough

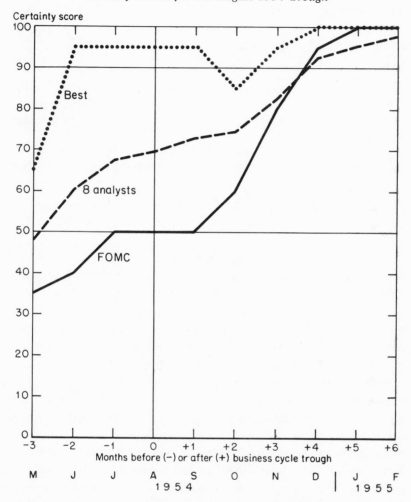

Certainty score

Months before (−) or after (+) business cycle trough

| M | J | J | A | S | O | N | D | J | F |
| | | | 1 9 5 4 | | | | | 1 9 5 5 | |

SOURCE: Part I of this study and other original data made available to the author.

way." [50] During August, the NBER trough date, the Committee stuck to its view that the economy was leveling off but saw some signs of improvement. The common view was that "the economy appears to be moving sidewise with some signs of improvement. . . . There is nothing

[50] *Ibid.,* July 7, 1954, pp. 208–209.

at present, however, to indicate a strong upsurge and modest seasonal increases this fall is the most likely outcome." [51] Again there was no change in the policy of active ease.

Although in September the economy started its upswing from the plateau on which it had been for the past several months, the Committee's view was much the same as before. Allan Sproul stated the typical view:

> We appear to have been on an economic plateau for the past three or four months following upon the decline in economic activity which began in the summer of 1953.
> I believe that a generally sidewise movement of the economy is more likely during the next few months than a pronounced and cumulative movement either up or down. [52]

The Committee members agreed that continued sidewise movement was the most likely prospect over the near term and decided to continue the existing policy of ease.

The Committee's outlook changed little by the October meetings. It agreed with R. A. Young's characterization of the situation as one of "high level doldrums." There were too few encouraging signs to indicate general revival and few signs of renewed recession. But increasing optimism concerning future economic activity was indicated at the November meeting, along with some concern about nascent speculation, and the certainty score increased to 80 (see Chart II-4). The Committee recognized the strengthening in the situation and doubted that the upward trend would be reversed. However, the members were not entirely convinced that cyclical expansion was already underway and did not change the policy of active ease.

At its December meetings, the Committee was virtually certain that a cyclical turn in business conditions had occurred and that revival was underway. Most of the Committee expressed agreement with Allan Sproul's assessment of the outlook:

> The economy seems definitely to have turned upward. . . . The danger in continuing to pursue the first course [aggressive ease] is that it might now encourage speculative forces in the economy which could lead to a brief burst of activity and another relapse.
> We are just coming into a recovery phase of economic activity, in which

[51] *Ibid.,* August 24, 1954, p. 245.
[52] *Ibid.,* September 22, 1954, pp. 277–278.

we want to avoid a false speculative upturn, but in which we also want to avoid nipping the bud of real recovery.[53]

R. A. Young pointed out that "data becoming available made it clear that a vigorous economic recovery was now visible and tangible." [54] And Chairman Martin thought that "recovery had a full head of steam." He doubted if the Federal Reserve was likely to do anything which could "nip the recovery in the bud." [55]

For the 1954 trough, the FOMC's certainty scores were the second highest of any turn—second only to scores in the vicinity of the 1949 trough. For the business analysts and the "best" of the eight, the certainty scores for this turn were the highest among any of the postwar turns.[56] Although both groups confirmed the occurrence of the trough in December, the business forecasters were substantially more optimistic through the second and third quarters when the Committee characterized the economy as moving sidewise. The performance of the "best" analyst is so good that it suggests an "optimistic" bias. For a comparison of these three performances see Chart II-4.

Flat or U-shaped turns in the direction of economic activity are inherently more difficult to recognize than sharp or V-shaped turns. The 1954 trough was flat bottomed which makes precise dating of the turn difficult and somewhat tenuous. If the present National Bureau business cycle date of August is taken as the date of the trough, the recognition performance of all forecasters studied is quite good. If recent revisions in data influence the NBER to move the trough to a period earlier in the year, perhaps May, June, or July, the performances will not look as good.[57]

As Chart II-4 shows, the certainty scores of the Committee are substantially below those of other forecasters for the months in the immediate vicinity of the trough. Perhaps this is a case where policy responsibility dampened the FOMC's optimism. As early as April, the Com-

---

[53] *Ibid.,* December 7, 1954, pp. 366–368.

[54] *Ibid.,* December 28, 1954, pp. 395–396.

[55] *Ibid.,* p. 403.

[56] See Part I, p. 29, and other original data made available to the author.

[57] For discussion of the NBER and alternative dates of cyclical turns, see: Lorman C. Trueblood, "The Dating of Postwar Business Cycles," *Proceedings of the Business and Economics Section of the American Statistical Association,* Washington, D. C., 1961; George W. Cloos, "How Good Are the National Bureau's Reference Cycle Dates?" *Journal of Business,* January 1963; and Victor Zarnowitz, "On the Dating of Business Cycles," *Journal of Business,* April 1963.

mittee was aware of the slackening in the pace of recessionary tendencies and correctly diagnosed the "leveling off" which occurred. However, there was not a significant increase in its certainty score until November, and cyclical expansion was not confirmed until December. It is apparent that the FOMC was wary of nipping possible recovery in the bud and this concern influenced its views during the extended period of sidewise movement.

5. The 1957 Peak

The recovery gained vigor in the early part of 1955 and the expansion proved to be one of the most exuberant on record. From the trough in GNP during the second quarter of 1954, the economy grew over the next thirty-five months to a peak GNP of $446.3 billion during the third quarter of 1957—an increase of over 20 per cent. The economy teetered on the brink of contraction throughout 1956. However, the boom in fixed investment by business and the revival of government expenditures helped to prevent cyclical contraction. The expansion resumed in the fourth quarter of 1956, sparked by the recovery from the steel strike, the increase in automobile production resulting from the introduction of new models, an increase in federal government expenditures, and a sharp increase in exports as a result of the Suez Crisis. However, the economy was unable to maintain the momentum, and the peak of the expansion came in July 1957 (with August a close runner-up).

Upon recognizing the revival in economic activity, the FOMC began tightening credit and continued to put pressure on the reserve position of member banks throughout 1955. Even though the Committee fluctuated between optimism and pessimism as to the rate of economic activity during 1956, at no time did it foresee a probability of deflationary forces gaining sufficient strength to carry the economy into recession.

At the beginning of 1957, the Committee characterized the economic situation as strong and still inflationary. The economy continued to operate at close to peak levels but seemed to be losing some of its momentum. During February there was increasing discussion of the possibility of a downturn sometime during the year, but the Committee felt that the evidence of weaknesses was not yet sufficient to justify a change in the policy of restraint. Its view was that the economy might be entering a period of sidewise movement at high levels.

No change in policy was made at the March or April meetings although the Committee noted that evidence of slackening continued to mount. The economic situation was pictured as one of activity on a "high plateau." The tenor of reports at the May meetings was little changed. The outlook continued uncertain; some economic indicators were edging up while others were drifting down. The Committee decided that the prudent course of action was to maintain the status quo and to wait until the outlook was clear before taking any policy action.

In its midyear outlook, the Committee judged that the economy continued to operate at high levels although moving sidewise, perhaps with a slight upward tilt. The majority of the FOMC felt that the most probable direction of activity was an upturn in the fall, with a concomitant increase in inflationary pressures. The Committee's August forecast was essentially the same. Although the discount rate was raised from 3 to 3.5 per cent between the July and August meetings, no change was made in open market policy or in the degree of restraint to be maintained in either month. The minutes summarized Chairman Martin's statement of the consensus as follows:

> With the seasonal demand coming on he would tend toward a $500–$400 million level of net borrowed reserves rather than risk getting up to $600 million or higher. . . . The discussion today made it clear in his opinion that there should be no change in the Committee's directive and no change in policy, and he subscribed to that point of view completely.[58]

The certainty score for August (40) reflects the view that the Committee did not think a peak probable and its discussion of policy indicated no desire to change the degree of restraint.

The FOMC detected little change in the trend of economic activity at its September meeting. Its view was that activity continued at high levels with offsetting adjustments. The members foresaw neither the formation of deflationary forces sufficient to cause a downturn nor a combination of forces which would lead to an upsurge of general demand pressures and greater inflationary pressures. Its minutes indicate that the Committee did not visualize a change in policy from continued restraint and that it had not "recognized" the peak. However, several

[58] *Minutes,* August 20, 1957, pp. 530–531.

members indicated that, because of the increased pessimism in the business and financial communities, the same degree of tightness could be achieved with a lower level of negative free reserves.[59] Chairman Martin's position, as summarized in the minutes, was that:

it was always necessary to resolve doubt one way or the other in carrying out Committee policy, and for the immediate future [until the current Treasury financing was completed] he would resolve these doubts on the side of ease rather than tightness.[60]

In October, there was a decided increase in pessimism. The staff stated that recent developments called for a thorough review of the economic situation, and that:

the economy as a whole showed basic strength but there was uncertainty as to what combination of demands would prevent recession in activity or, better, make for advance in total output and employment at present price levels.[61]

Other representative comments were:

Doubts as to the business outlook have been very considerably strengthened by developments since we met three weeks ago.

Statistical data for September and early October suggest that the business plateau which we have recognized for many months is beginning to tilt downward.[62]

Now that the marked upturn in fall business activity has not materialized, the time has come for adapting Federal Reserve System credit policy to an economic situation which indicates that general activity may be falling from its long heralded high plateau.[63]

However, not all members of the Committee shared the more pessimistic outlook. As Vice-Chairman Hayes summed it up:

There was a fairly even division between those who appraised the outlook with the view that statistics and developments that had been observed held a considerable threat of recession and those who felt that basically such a possibility was still to be demonstrated and that recent developments were largely psychological with the basic factors remaining strong.[64]

[59] *Ibid.,* September 10, 1957, pp. 547–557.
[60] *Ibid.,* pp. 570–572.
[61] *Ibid.,* October 22, 1957, pp. 615–618.
[62] *Ibid.,* pp. 619–622.
[63] *Ibid.,* pp. 630–631.
[64] *Ibid.,* p. 650.

These divergent views resulted in a decision to make no overt change in policy direction. The Committee's decision was that:

there was no immediate occasion to reverse its policy of restraint on credit expansion or to make a change in the policy directive. While it was clear that the Committee at this juncture did not wish to make any move which would signal a change in policy, it wished to supply seasonal needs reasonably freely. It did wish to increase restraint from what it had been. There was some feeling that the Committee should actually diminish restraint a little, but more of the members believed that the Committee should resolve doubts on the side of ease.[65]

At the November meeting, although all the members recognized that the economy was no longer on the "high plateau," not all of them were willing to call the downward trend the beginning of a cyclical contraction. Comments indicative of the two views were:

The most recently available data confirm that moderate downward adjustment has, in fact, been occurring. Indeed, the composite showing that cyclical downturn has now set in is fairly impressive.[66]

These changes had been desirable and in the direction that the Committee had been aiming for some time past in trying to bring the inflationary forces under control. There was still a strong possibility of a resurgence of upward pressures . . . and any overt move toward ease, any positive change in the direction of policy, would seem . . . to be a mistake at this time.[67]

There was no longer a question of forecasting a change in the economy; it was a question of recognizing what was on us.[68]

The policy consensus reached by the Committee was to moderate the pressure on bank reserves. It changed its directive for the first time since March 1957, and instructed the account manager to conduct operations with a view to "fostering sustainable growth in the economy without inflation, by moderating the pressures on bank reserves." [69] The *Minutes* clearly indicate that this was the first overt action taken in the direction of ease as a result of anticipated economic trends. Prior to this action, policy changes had been slight modifications within the continuing policy of restraint. In November the policy of restraint itself was abandoned. Such a decisive change was in keeping with the

[65] *Annual Report of the Board of Governors of the Federal Reserve System, 1957*, p. 54.
[66] *Minutes*, November 12, 1957, pp. 660–662.
[67] *Ibid.*, pp. 690–691.
[68] *Ibid.*, pp. 671–674.
[69] *Annual Report of the Board of Governors of the Federal Reserve System, 1957*, pp. 54–55.

rise in the certainty score from 55 to 85. The minor adjustments in policy made in the previous three months reflect the FOMC's response to a slowly changing assessment of the outlook.

Despite the policy change that occurred in November, it was not until the December meetings that the Committee was definitely convinced that a cyclical downturn had occurred and that the economy was in a recession. R. A. Young's statement typifies the Committee's outlook:

> In recent reports to the Committee, I have used the words "downsettling" to characterize the drift in over-all activity. In the light of recent information, general economic recession now appears to be the most appropriate description.[70]

Thus it was some five months after the July peak before the FOMC "confirmed" the contraction as a cyclical one.

Among peaks, the FOMC's certainty scores for 1957 are second only to those for 1953. The same is true for the business analysts. The recognition patterns of the two groups are strikingly similar, although the Committee was somewhat more pessimistic during the period of sidewise movement. Both groups indicated significant increases in the degree of recognition in November, after the President's comment that the economy was taking a breather. To account for the business forecasters' poorer performance in recognizing the 1957 peak relative to the 1953 peak, Fels suggested that "inaccurate information" and the "persistence of inflation, in the form of rising consumer prices, after the cyclical peak was passed" were contributing factors.[71] These influenced the forecasts of the Committee as well, particularly the continued rise in the consumer price index. (See Chart II-5.)

Both the Committee and the average of the business analysts performed better than the "best" business forecaster. In this case, the latter's "optimistic bias" worked against it. Even four months after the peak, the publication did not view a recession as probable.

6. The 1958 Trough

The cyclical peak occurred during the third quarter of 1957. The recession that followed was the shortest but the most severe of the postwar

---

[70] *Minutes,* December 12, 1957, p. 770.
[71] See Part I, pp. 30–31.

CHART II-5

Certainty Scores for the July 1957 Peak

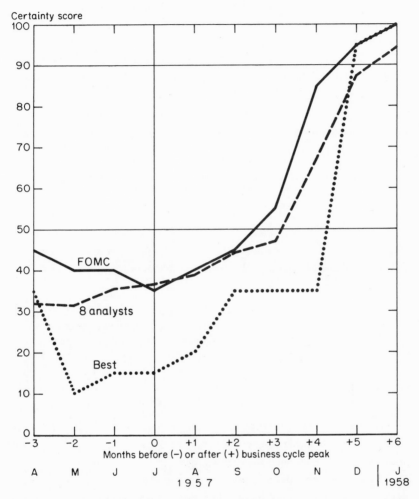

Certainty score

Months before (−) or after (+) business cycle peak

SOURCE: Part I of this study and other original data made available to the author.

period. Indeed, it was one of the shortest on record, lasting only nine months—from July 1957 to April 1958. Though brief, the contraction was sharp. GNP declined from $446.3 in 1957-III to $434.7 in 1958-I. Despite the decline in business activity, price levels generally continued rising during the contraction, so that in real terms the recession was even more severe. Unemployment rose from 3 per cent of the labor force at the peak of the expansion to a postwar high of 7.4 per cent a year later. The upturn came quickly. Early in 1958, the deflationary factors abated in strength and expansionary factors gained in force. According to the NBER chronology the trough occurred in April.

The Committee continued to ease credit during the first quarter of 1958. It had recognized the recession and was concerned about its length and depth. Virtually all economic indicators were continuing their downward trend and the outlook was for further contraction in activity. The comment characterizing the view of the majority in early March was that:

the most recent facts clearly suggest that the 1957–58 recession has a better than even chance of being less moderate in extent and duration than either the 1948–49 recession or the 1953–54 recession.[72]

In mid-April, the outlook was for continued decline in output and employment, but the Committee did see faint signs of some slowing down in the rate of decline and perhaps even some leveling off. The majority of the Committee felt that:

most recent data on recession are suggestive of some slowing down in the pace of decline for total output and employment, some leveling out in trade, and some developments of an expansive character in finance.

At the same time, the over-all drift is still plainly downward. Indeed, current figures offer only slight basis for hope that the saucering-out phase of recession is at hand, and very little, if any encouragement for hope that revival will be setting in within a score of weeks.[73]

A few members were substantially more optimistic than this statement indicates. For example, Governor Robertson stated that "he had a very definite feeling that the economy was getting ready to start upward." [74] To ease the market, the Committee, on balance, favored a reduction of the discount rate and a reduction in reserve requirements in lieu of open market purchases. These actions were taken.

The Committee became more optimistic during its meetings in May. The talk of a leveling-off and a recovery increased. Many of the economic indicators suggested that the recession might be "saucering out" but

---

[72] *Minutes,* March 4, 1958, pp. 170–173.
[73] *Ibid.,* April 15, 1958, pp. 269–270.
[74] *Ibid.,* p. 298.

there was no clear evidence of a general upswing. The majority opinion was that:

a bottom to decline in economic activity appears to be in the making.

But it is a long jump from the conclusion that recession may be bottoming out to the conclusion that recovery is shortly to begin.

On balance, it seems best to view the period which the economy is now entering as one of test of recession bottom.[75]

Governor Robertson again differed with the view of the majority. He advocated a policy formulated on the basis of a recovery rather than a leveling-off.[76] The Committee decided that there was no need for a change in policy or in the degree of ease.

By June the Committee was convinced that the recession was bottoming-out, but was undecided as to the length of the bottom and the timing of the recovery. The comment most representative of the FOMC's view was that:

Bottoming-out of recession is in fact occurring. It is the better part of wisdom *not* to conclude as yet that a recovery pattern has definitely taken form.[77]

Governor Robertson persisted in his optimism. To him "The economic report indicated very clearly a leveling out or possibly an upward movement." [78] Again the Committee made no change in the existing degree of ease to be maintained. Although there was no change in policy, their discussion of the outlook indicates that the Committee members thought the probability of cyclical recovery in June to be about 50-50 (see Chart II-6).

As July progressed, the Committee shifted its views of the situation from leveling-off to doubts about the nature of the recovery: temporary or permanent. Comments indicative of the doubtful nature of the rebound were:

Whether an abrupt turnabout of activity is taking place or *whether* evident improvement merely reflects a temporary rebound of production too far below consumption is yet to be determined.[79]

[75] *Ibid.*, May 27, 1958, pp. 377–379.
[76] *Ibid.*, p. 298.
[77] *Ibid.*, June 17, 1958, pp. 429–430.
[78] *Ibid.*, p. 434.
[79] *Ibid.*, July 8, 1958, pp. 472–473.

CHART II-6

Certainty Scores for the April 1958 Trough

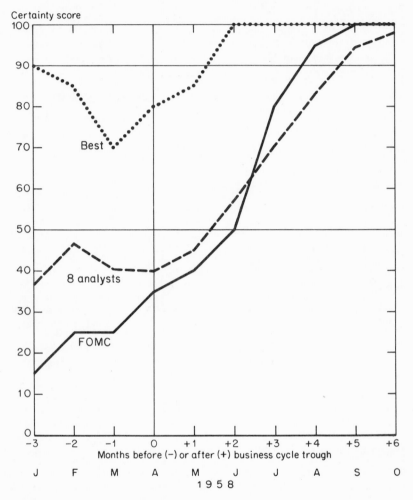

SOURCE: Part I of this study and other original data made available to the author.

The country was not yet in a vigorous recovery and there was still a possibility that the economy might be experiencing sort of a false bottom.[80]

By its last meeting in July, the evidence of business improvement was sufficient to cause the FOMC to change the direction of policy, although

[80] *Ibid.*, p. 501.

it was not completely confident that a cyclical upswing had indeed occurred and that the recovery was more than temporary. All the members' comments were hedged with such phrases as "looks as if," "increasingly clear," and "no conclusive evidence." For example, Young, in his staff review, pinpointed the turning point date but hedged just a bit: "domestically, springback of economic activity has been impressive, so much so that it now looks as if April will mark the recession trough and May the first month of revival." [81] Most of the other statements by Committee members were hedged with qualifications. In view of the evident improvement in business conditions, the Committee decided that the appropriate policy was to reduce the existing degree of ease by recapturing redundant reserves which had been injected into the market in early July to combat a "disorderly condition."

It was not until August that the Committee confirmed that the contraction was over and decided to move decisively in the direction of tightness. Only then was the policy directive changed to provide for open market operations with a view "to fostering conditions in the money market conducive to balanced economic recovery." [82] The Committee agreed that cyclical revival was underway and concurred with R. A. Young's statement that:

we no longer need to be tentative about the fact of domestic economic recovery. The unfolding data are abundantly clear. They show vigorous revival—one of the more robust on record following one of history's shorter and milder contraction periods.[83]

Among troughs, the Committee's certainty scores in the vicinity of the 1958 turn were the lowest. The same is true for the average score of the eight business analysts. Although the Committee recognized a change in the situation as early as April, and perceived the recovery in early July, it was not until August that it was confident that the recession was over. After experiencing two recessions which had rather flat bottoms, undoubtedly the Committee members were again expecting a "saucering out" rather than a sharp turn upward. Such an expectation would account for their reluctance to confirm that the recovery recognized in July was the cyclical trough.

Much the same pattern of recognition was followed by other fore-

[81] *Ibid.*, July 29, 1958, p. 590.
[82] *Annual Report of the Board of Governors of the Federal Reserve System, 1958*, p. 59.
[83] *Minutes*, August 19, 1958, p. 692.

casters (see Chart II-6). Again the performance of the "best" forecaster was remarkable, especially in comparison with the FOMC and the average of the eight analysts. One again suspects a strong optimistic bias.

7. The 1960 Peak

The expansion which followed the 1957–58 contraction was the shortest of the postwar expansions—twenty-five months. GNP in current dollars increased from its low of $434.7 billion in the first quarter of 1958 to a peak of $504.7 billion during the second quarter of 1960, a rise of some 15 per cent. In spite of the expansion, the economy never really approached full employment at any time during the recovery. The unemployment rate, which had risen above 7.5 per cent during the recession, never fell below 5 per cent during the upswing.

After August 1958 the FOMC tightened the pressure on reserves of member banks quickly and vigorously. By the end of the year free reserves had dropped from about $500 million to a negative $150 million. From a 1.75 per cent discount rate in mid-1958, the rate was moved up steadily until, at the beginning of 1960, it stood at a postwar high of 4 per cent. With but little variation the FOMC viewed the economy as expanding throughout 1959, and expected inflation to occur at almost any moment.

At its first meeting in 1960 the FOMC expressed confidence in the future outlook. The majority opinion was that "the customary measures of current activity are almost all up, and further increases seem as certain for the near term as anything can be." [84] The Committee's consensus was to continue the existing policy and it instructed the account manager to maintain the status quo.

[84] *Minutes,* January 12, 1960, pp. 6–7. Governor A. L. Mills was consistently less sanguine than the majority through the first quarter of the year. He dissented from the optimistic view and argued that:

The opening of the year 1960 reveals the national economy badly over-extended creditwise and finds the System's Open Market Committee faced with the necessity of conducting a monetary and credit policy that will prevent tautness in the credit markets from reaching the breaking point and still allow enough credit headroom to support stable and sustainable economic growth. The rationale of such policy argues that deflation is a more imminent danger than inflation, and that if a severe deflation is to be avoided economic momentum must be maintained through the invigorating impulse of a reasonable flow of newly created commercial bank credit into the economy. (*Ibid.,* pp. 31–32.)

By its second meeting in January, sufficient evidence had accumulated to indicate that the expected vigorous boom with accompanying inflationary pressures had not developed. The failure of the economy to meet these expectations introduced some uneasiness. While the Committee still felt that forces were on the side of expansion, some members expressed tentative doubts about the future level of activity. The consensus of the meeting was that an "even keel" should be maintained and that no change in the policy directive was called for.

The Committee continued to discount the poor performance of the economy at the February meeting. Its feeling was that the performance was bad only in relation to exuberant expectations. The majority opinion was expressed by Guy Noyes and Alfred Hayes. Noyes said, "The prospects for avoiding an inflationary boom are certainly brighter— and as is inevitably the case, the possibility that we may be confronted with a major readjustment is similarly enhanced." [85] Hayes also recognized the moderating tendency but stated, "I believe it would be a mistake, however, to over-emphasize these moderate tendencies, since the basic outlook for production, employment, and spending is strong, and the possibility of an inflationary boom cannot be dismissed completely while the year is yet so young." [86] The Committee's decision was that open market operations should be directed toward a "slight but not visible" easing.[87] The certainty score assigned was 30 (see Chart II-7).

At its meetings in March, the Committee expressed increasing concern about the future course of business activity, primarily because of the failure of new expansionary forces to appear. Typical statements describing the situation were:

On balance, the current business lull appears likely to represent a period of hesitation in a strong or expanding economy, rather than the beginning of a cumulative downward movement.[88]

The upward trend of activity seemed definitely to have slowed somewhat, but there were no signs of serious weakness.[89]

The country was in the midst of a lull before an outbreak of expansionary forces in the near future.[90]

[85] *Ibid.,* February 9, 1960, pp. 114–115.
[86] *Ibid.,* pp. 120–122.
[87] *Ibid.,* p. 168.
[88] *Ibid.,* March 22, 1960, pp. 267–268.
[89] *Ibid.,* pp. 276–277.
[90] *Ibid.,* p. 280.

CHART II-7

Certainty Scores for the May 1960 Peak

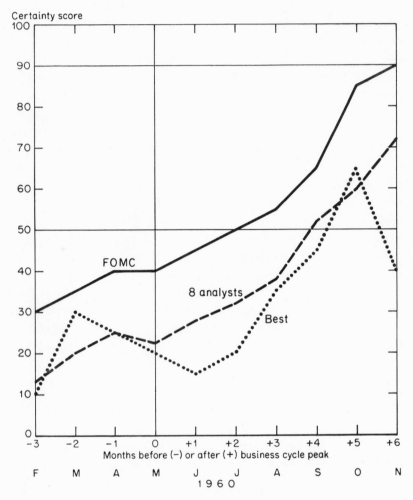

Certainty score

SOURCE: Part I of this study and other original data made available to the author.

The Committee agreed that its policy in the immediate future should be one of moderately less restraint and that open market operations should be conducted with a view "to fostering sustainable growth in economic activity and employment while guarding against excessive credit expansion." [91] The statements cited above indicate that the FOMC was fully aware of a slowing down in activity but did not anticipate the beginning of a cyclical contraction.

The April economic outlook was still uncertain, but fears of a cyclical downturn were not expressed. The statement that most closely characterized the Committee's position came from Governor Balderston, who stated that "the situation at the moment seemed to be one that might be described as 'rolling prosperity.' Whether it was rolling uphill, on the level, or downhill, he did not know . . ." [92] The meeting resulted in a consensus to move in the direction of slightly more ease but with great care that this not be done in an overt way so that no one would get the impression that the Committee was more concerned about the future outlook than it really was. The minutes made it clear that the Committee was fully cognizant of the deteriorating economic condition but that it was not convinced that the deflationary forces were cyclical in nature. The certainty score assigned was 40.

During May, the NBER peak month, the Committee members voted to move toward zero free reserves—another move in the direction of ease. They characterized this action as "leaning against the wind" when, as they viewed the situation, there was no deflationary or inflationary wind to lean against. A zero level of free reserves was considered to be a neutral policy which was appropriate to a view that the economy was undergoing a moderate expansion with no evidence of inflation. Comments indicative of this view were:

Although economic activity is at a relatively high level and will probably continue its expanding trend, the expansion is likely to be moderate . . .[93]

The most recent business information indicates the probability of a moderate expansion in business activity.[94]

The chances were greater that the economy would move upward than it would move downward.[95]

This outlook was shared with varying degrees of confidence by most of the Committee members. The minutes show that the policy change was not taken in anticipation of a cyclical contraction.

The Committee's outlook was a little less optimistic in June. The

[91] *Ibid.*, March 1, 1960, pp. 252–253.
[92] *Ibid.*, April 12, 1960, pp. 357–359.
[93] *Ibid.*, May 3, 1960, pp. 389–392.
[94] *Ibid.*, pp. 394–395.
[95] *Ibid.*, pp. 404–406.

indicated by the following short phrases from their appraisals of the outlook: "depth and duration of the recession," "there was little evidence to support anything other than a pessimistic view," "little cheerful news," "recessionary economic influences," "signs of further weakening," and "sliding-off of activity." Perhaps Chairman Martin's statement best characterizes the Committee's view of the situation:

> There was a declining business picture, whether it be called a recession or a rolling adjustment, but the economy was not going over a precipice by any means. There was no sign as yet that the decline had burgeoned into a major depression. There had been recessionary tendencies since March . . .[106]

Its discussion makes it evident that the Committee wished to continue the easy money policy.

In November, the Committee confirmed the existence of recession. Guy Noyes, in summarizing the staff report, stated:

> For what it is worth, the evidence of future plans suggests that the further declines will be less precipitous than any other postwar downturn.
>
> Certainly, the downward drift in the economy so far is not the sort of decline that has generally been associated with a recession in business cycle analysis. It has led to a profusion of new and refurbished descriptive phrases—and I can see no harm in offering still another. I would like to suggest that this might be termed a "moderated recession." [107]

The Committee agreed with the staff's analysis of the situation and the policy pursued was continued ease. Thus the "confirmation lag" at the 1960 peak was six months.

For the Committee, certainty scores in the vicinity of the 1960 peak were the second lowest among all turns. For the average of the eight business analysts and for the "best" analyst, the performance was the poorest among all turns, peaks or troughs. Although their recognition patterns are quite similar, the Committee "recognized" and "confirmed" the peak well before the other forecasters (see Chart II-7). Perhaps some of the FOMC's superiority can be accounted for by quicker access to the relevant economic data. However, here the Committee simply seems to have been the best forecaster.

A number of factors account for the relatively poor performances in recognizing the cyclical nature of the deterioration in business condi-

---

[106] *Ibid.*, October 25, 1960, p. 837.
[107] *Ibid.*, November 22, 1960, pp. 859–861.

tions. Because of the extreme mildness of the decline in GNP (from $504.7 billion in 1960-II to $503.3 billion in 1960-IV), it is little wonder that the Committee hesitated to confirm the existence of recession. Characterizing the situation as "idling in neutral," "sidewise at a high level," etc., was not wholly inappropriate. An additional factor working against early "recognition" and "confirmation" may have been the decision to ease prior to the turn. As early as February, policy was changed to a "slight but not visible" easing and the degree of ease was continually increased through the next several months. Consequently the Committee was not under real pressure to recognize the peak and reverse the direction of policy.

8. Summary

OVER-ALL PERFORMANCE

A useful way to evaluate the Committee's performance in forecasting and recognizing cyclical changes in business conditions is to compare its recognition pattern with that of other forecasters. The recognition patterns of the FOMC and the mean patterns of the eight business analysts analyzed by Fels are quite similar. At only two turns, the 1949 trough and the 1960 peak, did the recognition and confirmation lags of the two groups differ significantly. In the case of the 1949 trough, the recession was double-bottomed and the Committee recognized the first turn as the true bottom. In 1960, the FOMC seems to have had a greater appreciation of the deflationary forces at work and, consequently, made better forecasts than the business publications.

For the most part, the cyclical turns which the Committee and the business analysts found easy or difficult to recognize were the same (see Table II-2). For both groups the troughs of 1949 and 1954 were the most readily recognized of all turns; the peaks of 1948 and 1960 the most difficult. There is a striking similarity in the rankings of the average certainty score for each turn between the two groups. This similarity holds if each turn is ranked among all turns and if the peaks and troughs are ranked separately.

Both the Committee and the business analysts consistently recognized and confirmed the occurrence of troughs more promptly than peaks (see Charts II-8, II-9, and II-10). At the four peaks studied, the FOMC achieved a mean certainty score of over 50 after a lag of two

TABLE II-2

Comparison of Recognition and Confirmation Lags Between the FOMC and Business Analysts

NBER Business Cycle Date	Rank of Average Certainty Score (high to low)[a]			Recognition Lag (months)			Confirmation Lag (months)		
	FOMC	Eight Business Analysts	Best Over-All	FOMC	Eight Business Analysts	Best Over-All	FOMC	Eight Business Analysts	Best Over-All
Peaks									
November 1948	7 (4)	6 (3)	5 (2)	+3	+2	+4	[b]	[b]	+4
July 1953	3 (1)	4 (1)	3 (1)	+2	+2	−3	+6	+6	+1
July 1957	4 (2)	5 (2)	6 (3)	+3	+4	+5	+5	+6	+5
May 1960	6 (3)	7 (4)	7 (4)	+3	+4	+5	+6	[b]	[b]
Troughs									
October 1949	1 (1)	2 (2)	4 (3)	−1	0	−2	+1	+6	+3
August 1954	2 (2)	1 (1)	1 (1)	+2	−2	−3	+4	+4	−2
April 1958	5 (3)	3 (3)	2 (2)	+3	+2	−3	+4	+5	+2

SOURCE: Rendigs Fels, Part I of this volume, and other original data made available to the author. Note that for the recognition lag of the "best over-all" forecaster there are three entries of − three months. Since Fels' scores only start at − three months, the author read the "best" forecaster's comments in earlier months to check if its recognition lag was shorter. For the 1953 peak, a − three-month lag is appropriate. However, for both the 1954 trough and the 1958 trough, the date of recognition was at − four months.

[a] Rank in parentheses is the rank (from high to low) of that turn among only the peaks or only the troughs. The prior ranking is among all turns.

[b] The turn was not confirmed within six months of the NBER reference cycle date.

CHART II-8

FOMC Certainty Scores for Postwar Peaks and Troughs

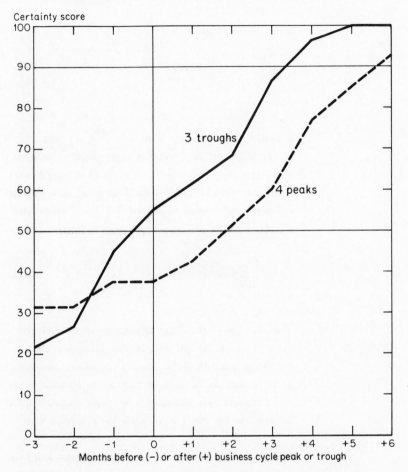

Certainty score

3 troughs

4 peaks

Months before (−) or after (+) business cycle peak or trough

SOURCE: Part I of this study and other original data made available to the author.

months; a mean score of 90 or better after a lag of six months. The eight business analysts, taken as an average, exceeded a mean score of 50 three months after the peaks; a mean score of 90 was not achieved even after the lapse of six months (see Chart II-9). At the three troughs studied, the FOMC achieved a mean certainty score of 55 with a zero lag; a mean score of 90 or better after a four-month lag. The eight

CHART II-9

FOMC and Business Analysts Certainty Scores for Four Postwar Peaks

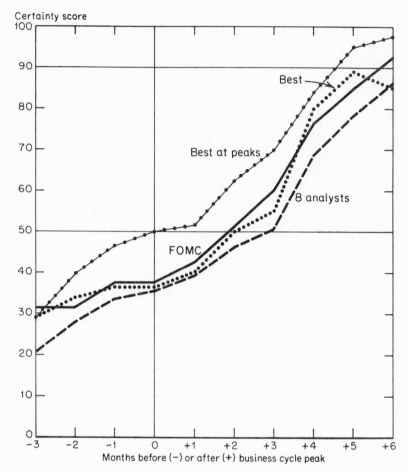

SOURCE: Part I of this study and other original data made available to the author.

business publications exceeded a mean score of 50 one month prior to the troughs; a mean score of 90 or better after a five-month lag (Chart II-10).

Taking the seven peaks and troughs together, a procedure that tends to compensate for any optimistic or pessimistic bias, the FOMC achieved an average certainty score of 27 per cent three months before the

CHART II-10

FOMC and Business Analysts Certainty Scores for
Three Postwar Troughs

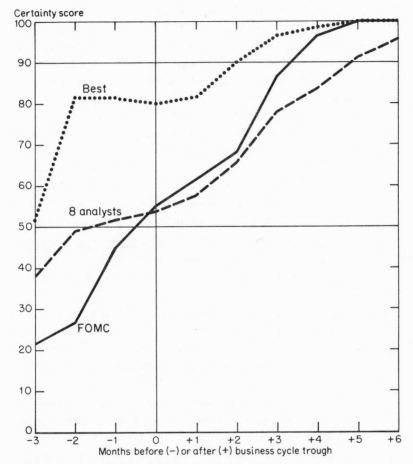

Certainty score

Best

8 analysts

FOMC

Months before (−) or after (+) business cycle trough

Source: Part I of this study and other original data made available to the author.

turn, 45 per cent at the turn, 71 per cent three months after the turn, and 96 per cent six months after the turn. The corresponding average figures for the eight business publications are nearly the same, namely: 28 per cent, 43 per cent, 63 per cent, and 90 per cent.

What accounts for the systematic difference in the recognition patterns for peaks and troughs? In the case of the FOMC, a contributing factor may have been that, until the Accord in 1951, its hands were virtually tied when it came to fighting inflation. The minutes indicate that during 1947–50 the Committee was more concerned with halting inflation, current and expected, than with insuring growth and full employment. It was during this period that the FOMC turned in its worst performance for recognizing a peak and its best performance for recognizing a trough. Its striving to disentangle itself from the responsibility for supporting government security prices impressed upon the FOMC the difficulties of combating inflation.

The dominant reason, however, seems to be that postwar peaks were inherently more difficult to recognize than troughs. In addition, historically, expansions have been more variable in length than have contractions. Since this is well known and expected by forecasters, they are continually on the lookout for the end of contractions but not for expansions.[108] As Fels suggested, forecasters were continually optimistic about the depth and duration of postwar recessions:

> Despite the forebodings of an occasional prophet of doom, forecasters have generally expected each contraction to be short and mild. Although they were not able to pinpoint when the trough would come, they were basically right.[109]

This optimism is particularly evident in the recognition pattern of the "best" forecaster (compare Charts II-11, II-12, and II-13). The FOMC may also have been optimistically "biased." As Guy Noyes, of the Committee's staff, suggests, "Perhaps this line of thinking proves only that Americans are incurable optimists, but there is some historical precedent for 'sidewise movements' that are fully recognized as 'recessions' only in retrospect." [110] Whatever the reason(s), there was a systematic difference in recognition patterns between peaks and troughs.

PERFORMANCE AT PEAKS

The Committee reached a mean certainty score of at least 50 two months after the NBER dates of the peaks; a mean score of 90 or better six months afterwards. The business publications exceeded a mean score of 50 three months after the peaks; a mean score of 90 was not reached within six months afterwards.

---

[108] I am indebted to Phillip Cagan of the National Bureau for this point.
[109] See Part I, p. 47.
[110] *Minutes*, September 13, 1960, p. 699.

CHART II-11

Certainty Scores at Seven Business Cycle Turns: FOMC

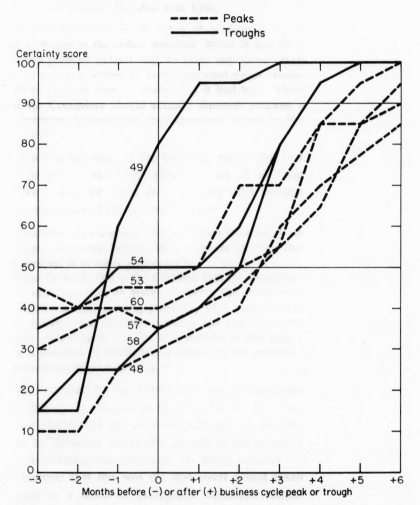

SOURCE: Part I of this study and other original data made available to the
author.

If the certainty scores in the vicinity of the four peaks are averaged,
there is little difference between the Committee's performance and that
of the eight publications (see Chart II-9). Over-all, the Committee
did little if any better than the average of the eight. Despite this similarity

CHART II-12

Certainty Scores at Seven Business Cycle Turns:
Mean of Eight Analysts

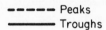

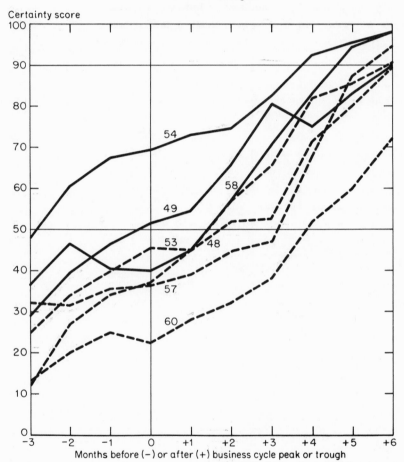

SOURCE: Part I of this study and other original data made available to the author.

CHART II-13

Certainty Scores at Seven Business Cycle Turns:
"Best" of Eight Analysts

– – – – – Peaks
———— Troughs

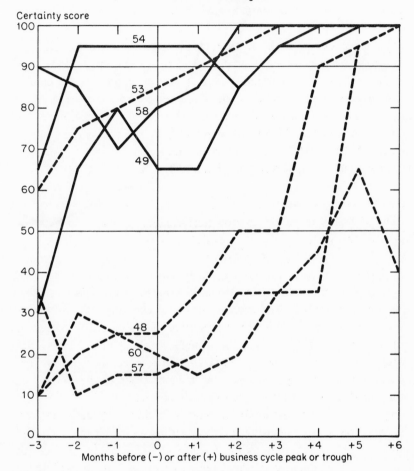

Certainty score

Months before (−) or after (+) business cycle peak or trough

SOURCE: Part I of this study and other original data made available to the
author.

in mean performances, there were substantial differences at each of the four peaks (see Charts II-1, II-3, II-5, and II-7). If the performances at peaks are reviewed individually, the Committee has generally succeeded in "recognizing" and "confirming" the turns prior to other forecasters (see Table II-2). However, only in the vicinity of the 1960 peak was the FOMC's recognition performance unambiguously superior to the business analysts'.

The forecaster with the highest mean certainty score for all turns taken together was not substantially better than the average of the eight together (Chart II-9). Actually there is little to choose in the over-all performances at peaks between the Committee and the average of the eight business analysts. Although the mean recognition pattern of the publication with the best record of recognizing peaks was quite similar to that of the FOMC, it succeeded in "recognizing" and "confirming" the turns one month before the Committee (Chart II-9).

PERFORMANCE AT TROUGHS

The FOMC's mean recognition performance in the vicinity of the three troughs is more difficult to evaluate. It achieved a mean score of over 50 with a zero lag; a mean score of 90 or better after a four-month lag. The eight business analysts taken together exceeded a mean score of 50 one month prior to the troughs; a mean score of 90 or better after a five-month lag. The average degree of certainty achieved by the eight analysts was substantially higher than the Committee's before the troughs, about the same from the troughs to about two months afterwards, and then lower (see Chart II-10). In essence, the business forecasters, on the average, "recognized" troughs prior to the FOMC but "confirmed" their occurrence after the Committee.

Again, the mean performances hide individual differences between the two groups in recognizing the three troughs (see Charts II-2, II-4, and II-6). However, only in the vicinity of the 1949 trough was the recognition performance of the Committee clearly the better. At the other troughs, the differences in recognition patterns are similar to those exhibited by their mean patterns.

In the case of troughs, the "best" forecaster was significantly better in its over-all performance than both the eight analysts and the FOMC. Its average recognition lag was — three months, its average confirmation lag, + two months (see Chart II-10). Indeed, its performance in recognizing troughs was so good that it is doubtful that forecasting ability accounts for it. The "best" forecaster is the publication with the highest mean recognition score for peaks and troughs taken together. Since it was only the fourth best performer at peaks, its performance at troughs primarily accounts for the high over-all certainty score. In fact, it had the highest mean certainty score at each of the three troughs.[111] Because of the difference in its performance at peaks and at troughs, one suspects a strong optimistic bias.

SUMMARY

In summary, both the Committee and the business analysts consistently recognized and confirmed the occurrence of troughs more promptly than peaks. The over-all recognition patterns of the FOMC and the other forecasters, taken as a group, are quite similar. At peaks there is little difference between the recognition patterns of the Committee and the average of the eight; at troughs, the business forecasters were better in giving early warning but the Committee was better in confirming their occurrence. All in all, the Committee's ability to forecast and recognize postwar cyclical turning points "can only be regarded as splendid," [112] if one assumes the same is true for other forecasters.

4

The FOMC's Recognition Pattern and Policy Decisions

The two previous studies of the Federal Reserve Board's ability to recognize and act on cyclical turns disagreed on conclusions. This was due to their widely different estimates of the Board's ability to recognize peaks; their results at troughs were of the same general nature. Both

---

[111] Fels, unpublished data.

[112] Brunner and Meltzer, *The Federal Reserve's Attachment to the Free Reserve Concept,* p. 50.

studies inferred recognition of cyclical turns from "policy changes." The results of such a procedure can be misleading. Additional insight into the actions of the monetary authorities is gained by determining the Federal Open Market Committee's ability to recognize cyclical turns independently of its policy decisions. In their studies, Kareken and Solow and Brunner and Meltzer realized that the date of recognition may not be equivalent to the date of policy change. Kareken and Solow thought that "insofar as the Federal Reserve is concerned, troughs signal the need for action, but peaks do not, or may not . . ." [113] Brunner and Meltzer apparently believed that peaks signal the need for action but that troughs may not. They wrote that "The fact that the lag in changing policy at troughs is longer than the lag at peaks does not necessarily indicate a slower recognition of recoveries. It is doubtful that more rapid movement toward 'restraint' would be desirable from the viewpoint of either the FOMC or the economy." [114] Review of the Committee's actions in the context of its views of past, current, and expected economic conditions (i.e., its recognition pattern) provides new information on the subject.

This section compares the certainty scores, which reflect the Committee's view of economic conditions, with the Brunner-Meltzer scores of policy action reflecting the direction and magnitude of the Committee's policy decisions. The general relationship between the two sets of scores is shown in Table II-3. Brunner and Meltzer scored all the FOMC's policy actions, as given in the "Record of Policy Actions" section of the Federal Reserve Board's Annual Reports. Table II-3 lists all those policy changes and the appropriate Brunner-Meltzer score which were made in the vicinity (minus three to plus six months) of

[113] Kareken and Solow, *Stabilization Policies,* p. 70.
[114] Brunner and Meltzer, *The Federal Reserve's Attachment,* p. 46.

Notes to Table II-3

SOURCE: Brunner and Meltzer, *An Alternative Approach to the Monetary Mechanism,* pp. 119–124.

    [a] The author argues in the text that these scores do not properly reflect the nature of the action taken by the FOMC. Specifically, the action in June 1953 was taken to counteract an anticipated disorderly market; the May 1958 action was again in response to prospective Treasury Financing difficulties; and the actions in July 1958 were taken to absorb reserves which had been previously injected to combat a disorderly market in government securities.

TABLE II-3

FOMC Policy Changes and Certainty Scores in the Vicinity of Postwar Turns

Month of Policy Change	Brunner-Meltzer Score	Certainty Score
November 1948 Peak		
March 1949	$+^{1}/_{2}$	70
April 1949	$+^{1}/_{8}$	77.5
May 1949	$+^{1}/_{2}$	85
October 1949 Trough		
November	$-^{1}/_{2}$	95
March 1950	$-^{1}/_{4}$	100
July 1953 Peak		
June	$+1$ [a]	45
September	$+^{1}/_{2}$	70
December	$+^{1}/_{2}$	85
August 1954 Trough		
December	$-^{1}/_{2}$	95
January 1955	$-^{1}/_{2}$	100
July 1957 Peak		
August	$+^{1}/_{8}$	40
September	$+^{1}/_{8}$	45
October	$+^{1}/_{4}$	55
November	$+^{1}/_{2}$	85
December	$+^{1}/_{2}, +^{1}/_{4}$	95
January 1958	$+^{1}/_{4}$	100
April 1958 Trough		
May	$-^{1}/_{8}$ [a]	40
July	$-^{1}/_{4}, -^{1}/_{4}$ [a]	80
August	$-^{1}/_{2}$	95
May 1960 Peak		
February	$+^{1}/_{8}$	30
March	$+^{1}/_{4}$	35
April	$+^{1}/_{2}$	40
May	$+^{1}/_{4}, +^{1}/_{2}$	40
June	$+^{1}/_{2}$	45
August	$+^{1}/_{4}$	55
September	$+^{1}/_{8}$	65
October	$+^{1}/_{8}$	85

peaks and troughs, along with the certainty score for the month in which the policy decision was made.

Although the Committee reversed the direction of policy quicker at peaks than at troughs, it did so at significantly lower certainty scores. The Committee was apparently willing to accept a greater degree of uncertainty when acting in the vicinity of peaks than at troughs. It switched toward easy money before "confirming" that a turn in general business had occurred at each of the four postwar peaks (see Table II-4). The Committee's decision-making process proceeded by successive approximations. At the peaks of 1953, 1957, and 1960, the FOMC made minor adjustments in the degree of restraint even before it was convinced that signs of leveling off and slowing down were indicative of general recession (see Table II-3). This seems prudent. Because of its power to act quickly and to make small adjustments, the Committee can afford to act without waiting to be sure that changing business conditions are auguries of a cyclical peak. In the vicinity of the postwar troughs, the Committee did not switch toward tight money until they were virtually certain that cyclical recovery was actually underway (see Table II-5). Again, this seems prudent. In the vicinity of troughs, the emphasis in monetary policy is on encouraging cyclical expansion. Even if the Committee confirmed troughs with a zero lag, it is doubtful that policy should be changed immediately upon "confirmation." In only one case—the 1958 upswing—did the Committee act before "confirming" the trough. And whether to regard the July decision "to recapture redundant reserves" as a reversal of policy is a marginal decision.[115] If the decisive action to tighten in August is assumed to be the date of policy reversal, the pattern of action only after "confirmation" of cyclical revival holds. In either case, the degree of recognition was greater than when policy was changed at any of the peaks. According to Brunner and Meltzer, the Federal Reserve indicated a desire to change policy at peaks after an average lag of a quarter of a month, and twice (in 1953 and 1960) changed policy prior to the approaching peak. Even ignoring the first change in 1953, which was in anticipation of a disorderly market,[116] the mean lag is still only a month. The mean certainty score when policy was first changed was about 45 per cent, ranging from 70 to 30. The first major change in policy at peaks, according to Brunner

[115] See Chapter 3 above.
[116] See Chapter 3 above.

TABLE II-4

Summary of FOMC Policy Changes and Certainty Scores

NBER Reference Cycle Date	Scale of First Indicated Desire to Change Policy [a]	Certainty Score at First Change	Lag [b] (in months)	Score of Major Change in Policy [a]	Certainty Score at Major Change	Lag [b] (in months)
Peaks						
November 1948	+1/2	70	+4	+1/2	70	+4
July 1953 [c]	+1 (+1/2)	45 (70)	-1 (+2)	-1 (+1/2)	45 (70)	-1 (+2)
July 1957	+1/8	40	+1	+1/4	55	+3
May 1960	+1/8	30	-3	+1/4	35	-2
Average for peaks [c]	+7/16 (+5/16)	46.25 (50.25)	+0.25 (+1)	+1/2 (+3/8)	51.25 (57.5)	+1 (+1.75)
Troughs						
October 1949	-1/2	95	+1	-1/2	95	+1
August 1954	-1/2	95	+4	-1/2	95	+4
April 1958	-1/8	40	+1	-1/2	95	+4
Average for troughs	-3/8	76.66	+2	-1/2	95	+3

[a] Brunner and Meltzer, *An Alternative Approach to the Monetary Mechanism*, pp. 119–124, and *The Federal Reserve's Attachment to the Free Reserve Concept*, p. 42.
[b] Minus means before Peak or Trough, plus after.

[c] For this row the score at time of change was made in anticipation of disorderly market. Number in parentheses pertains to change in policy in recognition of cyclical turn.

TABLE II-5

FOMC Average Certainty Scores at Dates of Policy Changes

Peaks			Troughs		
Brunner-Meltzer Score (1)	Number of Policy Changes (2)	Average Certainty Score (3)	Brunner-Meltzer Score (4)	Number of Policy Changes (5)	Average Certainty Score (6)
$1/8$	7	53.9	$-1/3$	1 [a]	40
$1/4$	6	63.3	$-1/4$	3	86.7
$1/2$	8	71.3	$-1/2$	4	96.3
1	1 [a]	45.0	-1	0	–

Source of cols. 1, 2, 4, and 5: Brunner and Meltzer, *An Alternative Approach,* pp. 119–124.

[a] The author argues in the text that these scores were inappropriate and do not properly reflect the Committee's actions.

and Meltzer, averaged about two months after the turns; the average degree of certainty was about 50 and the range was 70 to 35. (See Table II-4.)

For the three troughs studied, there was an average lag of two months before the Federal Reserve first indicated a desire to change the direction of policy. In the months of such changes, the mean certainty score was about 75, ranging from 95 to 40. Major changes in policy were made after an average lag of three months; the certainty score for each major change was 95. (See Table II-4, columns 4, 5, and 6.)

The Committee changed policy in the direction of ease about three times as often as it switched policy toward tightness. There were twenty-two policy actions at peaks, seven of which were minor. There were only eight actions taken at troughs, one of which was minor. (See Table II-5.) For both peaks and troughs, the more decisive the action taken, the greater the mean certainty score. The mean certainty score achieved by the Committee at the time of major changes in the direction of ease was substantially lower than the mean score achieved when changes were made in the direction of tightness. (See Tables II-4 and II-5.)

This general relationship between the Brunner-Meltzer scores and the certainty scores indicates that the Committee changed policy at peaks on less conclusive evidence than it required at troughs, and that its decision-making process in the vicinity of peaks proceeded by successive approximations. Given that, on the average, decisions to ease are made at lower certainty scores than decisions to tighten, this indicates that signs of a probable peak signal the "need for action" while signs of recovery do not. The Committee switched to tightness only after conclusive evidence was available that cyclical recovery was underway and only after being convinced that its action would not "nip the recovery in the bud." But at peaks, the Committee attempted to stimulate economic activity upon signals indicative of a probable recession, without waiting to be sure that changing business conditions were cyclical in nature.

5

Conclusions

Utilizing the Federal Open Market Committee's discussions of business conditions as given in its minutes, this study has assessed the ability of the Committee to anticipate and recognize cyclical peaks and troughs between 1947 and 1960. A scoring system developed by Rendigs Fels for evaluating forecasts was used to quantify the Committee's views of future economic conditions. Beginning three months before the NBER dates of postwar business cycle peaks and troughs and ending six months afterward, the FOMC's forecasts were scored. These scores represent an estimate of the probability of a cyclical turn implicit in the Committee's discussion of business conditions. The scores for this ten-month period are called the recognition pattern and they indicate the Committee's ability to recognize a cyclical turn as it is approached and then passed.

From this pattern of scores, two characteristics have been selected as being particularly useful for evaluating the FOMC's forecasts. The period between the date of a turn and the time when the Committee first indicates that it believes a turn is more likely than not is defined as the recognition lag. The period between the date of the turn and the time when the Committee first indicates that it is virtually certain that a turn has occurred is defined as the confirmation lag.

Using these three concepts—the recognition pattern, the recognition lag, and the confirmation lag, the FOMC's forecasts were compared with those of the eight business analysts studied by Fels. Next, the Committee's policy decisions were related to its recognition pattern to determine the relationship between the Committee's views of economic conditions and its policy decisions.

This attempt to quantify the Committee's forecasts, to assess its ability to recognize cyclical turns, to compare its performance with that of other forecasters, and to relate its recognition pattern to its policy actions revealed the following:

1. The beginning date of the Committee's recognition pattern varied from one to nine months before the cyclical turn. The pattern at the four peaks (1948, 1953, 1957, 1960) generally began before that at the three troughs (1949, 1954, 1958). The two peaks (1953 and 1957) for which the pattern began earliest are those which both the Committee and the business publications found easiest to recognize. On the other hand, the ending of the recognition pattern varied from one to seven months after the turn, and the pattern for troughs ended before that of peaks. With the exception of the 1948 peak, the Committee was certain of the occurrence of a turning point within six months after the NBER date of the turn. At the date of the turn, the estimated probability was generally below 50; it reached the vicinity of 50 about two months after the turn.

2. The Committee's comments on the business outlook in the vicinity of cyclical turns exhibit the same general pattern as that found by Fels for the business publications: "As time goes by, analysts become increasingly aware of first the possibility, then the probability, and finally the certainty of a turning point." [117]

The over-all performance of the Committee in recognizing postwar turns is not particularly impressive when compared with that of other forecasters.[118] Its performance was about the same as the average performance of the eight business analysts. The Committee and the other forecasters had mean certainty scores in the vicinity of peaks which were strikingly similar. At troughs, however, the business analysts

[117] See Part I, p. 47.
[118] See, however, p. xvi above.

"recognized" turning points earlier than the Committee but "confirmed" their occurrence later.

3. The Committee has systematically been quicker to reverse the direction of policy at peaks than at troughs, but it did so at substantially lower certainty scores. At peaks, action was taken soon after the Committee became aware of the probability of a recession. At troughs, changes in policy were made only after the FOMC was virtually certain that cyclical recovery was underway.

4. The Committee's actions in the vicinity of peaks indicate the difficulties involved in the concept of an inside lag or recognition lag measured by a single number. The recognition of cyclical turns is a gradual process and monetary policy, being a highly flexible tool, can be slightly modified as the Committee's assessment of the outlook slowly changes. For example, in 1957 the Committee made slight adjustments in policy during both August and September (the peak occurred in July). Neither change was made primarily because of concern about an anticipated peak, yet the Committee was aware of changing business conditions and this awareness was probably a factor contributing to its decisions. A similar case occurred in 1953. In June, a month before the peak, the FOMC injected reserves into the market primarily because of an anticipated disorderly market in government securities. However, concern about the future direction of economic activity may have influenced the Committee's decision. Again, in 1960 the Committee began to change policy in the direction of ease three months before the NBER date of the peak and continued easing almost continuously for the next several months. What is more, the decision in February was made because the Committee recognized the deceleration in economic activity. However, the minutes show that the members were not anticipating the approaching downturn nor did they think a peak probable.

5. At both peaks and troughs, the more confident the Committee was that changing business conditions were cyclical in nature, the more decisive its action.

APPENDIX II

TABLE A

FOMC Certainty Scores in the Vicinity of Cyclical Turns
(number of months before (−) and after (+) the turn)

NBER Business Cycle Date	−3	−2	−1	0	+1	+2	+3	+4	+5	+6	Aver. (−3 to +6)	Aver. (−3 to 0)
Peaks												
November 1948	10	10	25	30	35	40	60	70	77.5	85	44.0	18.8
July 1953	40	40	45	45	50	70	70	85	85	95	62.5	42.5
July 1957	45	40	40	35	40	45	55	85	95	100	58.0	40.0
May 1960	30	35	40	40	45	50	55	65	85	90	53.5	36.3
Average, four peaks	31.3	31.3	37.5	37.5	42.5	51.3	60.0	76.5	85.0	92.5		
Troughs												
October 1949	15	15	60	80	95	95	100	100	100	100	76.0	42.8
August 1954	35	40	50	50	50	60	80	95	100	100	66.0	43.8
April 1958	15	25	25	35	40	50	80	95	100	100	56.5	25.0
Average, three troughs	21.7	26.7	45.0	55.0	61.7	68.3	86.7	96.7	100	100		
Average, four peaks and three troughs	27.1	29.3	40.7	45.0	50.7	58.6	71.4	85.0	91.8	95.7		

APPENDIX II

TABLE B

FOMC Certainty Scores for All Months: January 1947 Through December 1960

Year	Jan.	Feb.	Mar.	Apr.	May	June	July	Aug.	Sept.	Oct.	Nov.	Dec.
						November 1948 Peak						
1947	10	10	10	10	12.5[a]	15	12.5[a]	10	10	10	10	10
1948	10	15	15	10	10	10	10[a]	10	10	25	30	35
1949	**40**	**60**	**70**	**77.5**	**85**							
						October 1949 Trough						
1949						15	**15**[a]	**15**	**60**	**80**	**95**	**95**
1950	**100**	**100**	**100**[b]	**100**[b]								
						July 1953 Peak						
1950			5	10	na	25	20	5	5	5	5	5
1951	5	5	5	10	10	10	15	20	20	25	20	30[a]
1952	30[a]	40	37.5[a]	35	35	35	30	25	25	15	10	15
1953	15	20	30	**40**	**40**	**45**	**45**	**50**	**70**	**70**	**85**	**85**
1954	**95**											
						August 1954 Trough						
1954	**100**	25	20	30	**35**	**40**	**50**	**50**	**50**	**60**	**80**	**95**
1955	**100**	**100**										

(continued)

TABLE B (concluded)

July 1957 Peak

Year	Jan.	Feb.	Mar.	Apr.	May	June	July	Aug.	Sept.	Oct.	Nov.	Dec.
1955	25		5	5	10	10	10	10	10	10	10	10
1956	25	35	25	25	35	35	25	15	10	15	25	25
1957		**30**	**35**	**45**	**40**	**40**	**35**	**40**	**45**	**55**	**85**	**95**
1958	**100**											

April 1958 Trough

Year	Jan.	Feb.	Mar.	Apr.	May	June	July	Aug.	Sept.	Oct.	Nov.	Dec.
1958	15	25	25	35	**40**	**50**	**80**	**95**	**100**	**100**		

May 1960 Peak

Year	Jan.	Feb.	Mar.	Apr.	May	June	July	Aug.	Sept.	Oct.	Nov.	Dec.
1958	10	10	10	10	5	10	10	10	10	10	10	10
1959	15	10	10	10	10	10	10	10	15	20	15	15
1960	15	**30**	**35**	**40**	**40**	**45**	**50**	**55**	**65**	**85**	**90**	15

NOTE: The scores in boldface are those in the vicinity of the turns and were scored on the basis of a three-month target interval centered on the NBER date of the turn. All other scores are based on the probability of a turn within plus or minus six months of month for which the score was assigned.

a No meeting that month. Score is interpolated.
b No meeting that month. Score is carried forward.

APPENDIX II

TABLE C

Certainty Scores of Individual Comments at FOMC Meetings in the Vicinity of the 1960 Peak
(number of months before (−) and after (+) the peak)

Individual	−3	−2[a]	−1	0[a]	+1	+2[a]	+3	+4	+5[a]	+6
Staff										
A	25	30/40	50	45/55	50		50	80	90/95	100
B	25	30		25/		/50		80		
C						45/50		80		
Governors										
A	25	40/40	40	35/35	35	35/45		70	70/80	85
B	45	45/40	50	45/50	50	/75		75	90/90	90
C	20	20/20	25	30/	30			45	55/	
D	25	35	45	/45	70	80/	85	85	/85	85
E	15	20/15	10	35/40	40	40/45	45	70	70/90	100
F	20	25/30	25	35/30	55		50	60	60/60	65
G	20	30		55/	55	55/	35			

(continued)

TABLE C (concluded)

Individual	−3	−2 [a]	−1	0 [a]	+1	+2 [a]	+3	+4	+5 [a]	+6
Presidents										
A	15	20/35	40	30/30	30	25/35	50	50	60/65	85
B	15	20/35	35	40/40	50	50/50	60	70	/100	100
C	15	25/50	40	40/	45	50/60	50	80		95
D	15	25/35		/40	40	/55	55	55	55/80	80
E	15	20/25	35	35/40	40	45/50		60	60/65	65
F	20	25/25	35	40/40	45	40/45		55	55/	65
G	20	20/20	45	30/	55	50/	50	40	40/50	50
H	15	25/30	45	/35	35	50/55	55	65	75/80	80
I	15	30/25	40	35/35	35	35/40	40	40	55/70	65
J	25	25/25	40	35/30	35	/45	50	50	50/50	
K		30/25	45	/35	35	/50	40	55	55/75	
L		30/25	25	30/30	50	50	55	55	55/60	75
Average	21.1	28.5	33.5	37.3	43.4	48.3	51.3	62.2	68.6	80.3
Score for the FOMC as a whole	25	30	40	35	40	50	50	65	85	90

[a] Two meetings in that month; the first score is for the first meeting, the second for the last. The final average for these months is the mean of all comments made within the month.

Index

Rendigs Fels is professor of economics at Vanderbilt University and has been a member of the NBER staff since 1964. He received his M.A. from Columbia and his Ph.D. from Harvard. Mr. Fels' previous publications include: *American Business Cycles, 1865-1897* (University of North Carolina Press, 1959) and *An Introduction to Economics* (Allyn & Bacon, Inc., 1961).

C. Elton Hinshaw is assistant professor of economics at Vanderbilt University, from which he received his Ph.D. He is currently on a University assignment with the Vargas Foundation in Rio de Janeiro.